Praise for

"I have known Paula Dunn for many years and have always been impressed with her heart for ministry. She is uniquely gifted in sharing the overwhelming grace of God in our lives. I know that God has used her in big ways in the past, and I also know He will use her in even more significant ways in the future for the Kingdom."

—Jonathan Falwell
Pastor of Thomas Road Baptist Church
Lynchburg, VA

"Paula Dunn's story is a magnificent example of courage, redemption, grace, and completion. Her life is a mirror of her ministry...consistent Godly living. For as long as I have known her, Paula has always had a huge heart for those who are hurting, and she is always a gracious blessing to all she is around. She has a powerful message, but she doesn't just share it from the stage; she lives it."

—Charles Billingsley
Worship Leader at Thomas Road Baptist Church
Artist in Residence at Liberty University
Lynchburg, VA

"For years, we have brought Paula Dunn in to be a part of our National Business Conferences. Not only has she performed her music at our events, but she has also shared her inspirational messages with our business leaders. Paula has a dynamic story of rising above her circumstances and living out God's dreams for her life—a story that has had a powerful impact on many people within our organization."

—Steve Yager
Founders Crown Ambassador for Amway Global
Vice President, InterNet Services
Charlotte, NC

"It's been my privilege to know Paula Dunn since she was a student at Liberty University. Throughout the years, her story of overcoming loss and living out her dreams is a source of incredible encouragement to me. Paula's words have renewed my passion to dream big."

—Vernon Brewer
President/CEO of World Help
Lynchburg, VA

"Paula Dunn has inspired me as an individual as well as crowds all across America with her singing and speaking. She has always had wisdom beyond her years and has finally penned it with great points of humor for the world to read. Her heart has nothing but pure intentions for Him, and this book is His reward from her heart."

—Judi Hines
COO, International Missionary Advocate Personnel (iMap)
Founder of Elevate with Style, Chateau de Thieusies, Belgium
Boise, ID

DARE
to
SOAR

Rising Above Our Greatest Obstacles
to Live Beyond Our Wildest Dreams

PAULA DUNN

Fedd Books
401 Ranch Rd. 620 S, Ste. 250
Austin, TX 78734
www.thefeddagency.com

ISBN: 978-0-9907044-4-7
eISBN: 978-0-9907044-6-1
Library of Congress Control Number: 2014959074

Editing by Layce Smith
Cover by Brooke Boling
Photographs by Brooke Boling
Interior Design by Lauren Hall

Printed in the United States of America

First Edition 10 9 8 7 6 5 4 3 2 1

Table of Contents

I would like to dedicate this book to my parents, Joe and Gloria Young, who loved me as their own and gave me the chance to *Dare to Soar.*

A Letter from the Author

No one is more surprised than I am that you are reading this book! Never in my wildest dreams did I imagine God would take the story of a little girl who was rescued from a life of despair and use it to touch and impact lives! There's hardly a day that goes by when I don't think of where my life could have been if God had not intervened. But, that is exactly what God does. He takes the broken pieces of our lives and masterfully weaves them together to form a story of grace like no other.

We all have stories—real-life stories, stories of joys and triumphs, and stories of heartache and defeat. It's all part of this beautiful, yet messy thing called life. But what we do with these stories has the power to take us from merely surviving life to actually thriving and living far beyond the dreams we ever thought possible.

When our stories, our purposes, and our passions intertwine with the dreams of our hearts, we truly live the life we were meant to live. It's a life that goes beyond ourselves, a life that makes a difference.

Whether you are at the beginning of discovering your dream or just in need of encouragement to carry on, *Dare to Soar* was written for you! I may not know your name or the details of your life, but God does. And in His sovereignty, He brought this book into your life for a reason. My prayer is that it will be more than just a good read. I pray that it will inspire, encourage, and challenge you to live the dreams God has burned within your heart.

As I wrote this book, I knew it couldn't be just about my story. It had to be about YOURS! God created you for a very special purpose, and that purpose is something we will explore together over the next ten chapters as we examine our dreams and the obstacles that often stand in the way. What I am especially excited about is the "Dream Weaving" section at the end of each chapter. This is a place for you to internalize the message and make it come alive in your own life. I want to encourage you to take your time as you answer the questions and journal. There are no right or wrong answers and there is no judgment. You are free to be honest and real. This is your journey into the incredible dreams God has for you!

Oh, and one more thing. If at any point throughout this book you are feeling pushed a little out of your comfort zone, believe me, you are in good company! This whole "writing a book" thing was exactly that for me. As you will soon find out, I am a wife, a mom, a singer, a speaker, and you might as well add a flagrant perfectionist and overachiever to the list. Notice the word *author* was not on that list. Perhaps the thought of permanently baring my soul to the world was just a tad bit intimidating and downright scary, similar to what one might feel standing out in their driveway naked. (I know, crazy illustration, but it gets my point across.) But living out our dreams is not for the weak of heart. We must dig deep and rise above our greatest obstacles (which often can even be ourselves) in order to live beyond our wildest dreams. The adventure ahead is awesome, so let's not waste another minute! Grab a cup of coffee or tea and a pen, and let's dive in!

In Him,

Chapter 1

No White-Picket Fences

THINK BACK WITH ME THROUGH THE CORRIDORS OF time to the moment in your childhood when you first began to dream. Perhaps it was on the swing set in your backyard with your very best friend in the whole wide world, or maybe it was while you participated in a lively game of neighborhood kickball. Somewhere embedded in those carefree moments, many of us had the infamous conversation of what we wanted to be when we grew up. There were so many possibilities—a teacher, a singer, an athlete, a doctor, a mom. I remember telling people that I wanted to be a Christian cheerleader. (I'm not really sure what that is, but it's what I told everyone.)

How did we ever narrow our dreams down to one thing? The sky was truly the limit, and then we grew up. With twists and turns along the way, we soon faced the stark reality that life is not always easy, as we once thought, and dreams don't always come true.

1

What dreams did you have as a young child? Can you say that you are living in the center of your dreams? If not, what robbed you of the childlike anticipation of conquering the world?

Many a dream has been drowned out by the difficult storms of life—rejection, loss, and heartache (just to name a few). However, these storms do not have to define us. The choice is up to us whether we will live in defeat or rise above our circumstances with God's help and allow Him to use us in ways we never dreamed possible.

You might be reading this and already thinking, *Paula, that's great that you can be so happy and chirpy and talk about dreams. You've probably had this perfect life and nothing has ever gone wrong. If only you had my life…there is no way you would ever be able to dream.*

First, let me say that no one has a perfect life and there are no perfect white picket fences in my story either. In fact, you will have a front row seat to the story of my life in the next chapter—a story that includes loss, disappointment, and pain. You see, at some point we all face struggles. It's a part of life. If you haven't had a problem yet, hang on because it's coming.

I know, nothing like starting off a book with discouraging news! But hold on. I promise this book is all about good news— good news that we don't have to live stuck in the past and that there is more to life than just surviving our problems.

Even our pain can be a part of our purpose. Here's the key:

our circumstances do not have to define us, but how we respond to our circumstances determines the level of success we will experience in life. I believe that when we figure out what to do with what has happened in our lives, we can find our purpose and the dreams God has for us.

_____

Our circumstances do not have to define us, but how we respond to our circumstances determines the level of success we will experience in life.

_____

ONE DEFINING OPPORTUNITY

I remember that one pivotal summer when my dream began. At the age of fourteen, I was asked to sing at Happy "T" Ranch—a camp for teenagers in Rumney, New Hampshire—and I thought I'd died and gone to Heaven. Singing was (and still is) the passion of my heart. Since the age of four, day after day I sat at my little electric keyboard and made up songs about Jesus and life as I knew it, so you can only imagine the excitement I felt when I was invited to sing for an entire summer at this Christian camp.

Just the drive to the camp was an amazing experience. Miles and miles of picturesque lakes, towering pine trees, and breathtaking mountain passes captivated my heart and beckoned me to this peaceful sanctuary nestled in the White Mountains of New Hampshire. As I arrived, I immediately knew something was different about this place. There was something sacred. It seemed to be more than just a fun place for teens to come and hang out. What I would soon realize is that this was a place to meet with God.

My relationship with God began many years prior, at the age of four, when our next-door neighbor suddenly died. At the time, I had all kinds of questions: *What happened to him? Where did he go? Why would I never see him again?* It was explained to me that if our neighbor had received Jesus as his personal Savior and had a personal relationship with Him, then he went to Heaven when he died. I knew right then and there that I wanted to know where I was going when I died and that I wanted it to be in Heaven with Jesus. So, I prayed and confessed my sins and asked Jesus to forgive me and to be my Savior.

However, at the Happy "T" Ranch that summer, I began to learn and understand that being a Christian doesn't just mean we receive Jesus into our lives, for it is not supposed to end there. As the director of the camp challenged us to be "sold out" for Jesus, I began to look at my life and knew that, while I hadn't made bad and rebellious choices, God wasn't totally number one in my life, which is as heartbreaking to Him as if I were not committed at all. For the first time, I understood that there is no halfway with God; we are either completely in or out; we are either moving toward God or away from Him, and the choice must be made.

ONE DEFINING DECISION

Honestly, I was a little hesitant as I contemplated the choice to go all in for God. Maybe I had seen too many flannel graph missionary stories in Vacation Bible School, or maybe I was just worried that this kind of commitment might send me off into the jungles of Africa to live in a little hut with no electricity and where life as I knew it would be gone forever. But it was as if God spoke into my heart and assured me that, even if my future landed me somewhere outside my comfort zone, I would be fulfilled because I would be living in the center of His will, His plan, and His dream for my life.

So, I closed my eyes and whispered, "Okay, God. It's not much, but you can have my life and do whatever you want with it." Almost instantly, a peace washed over me in knowing that God had control of my life. After all, who better to control my life than the God of the universe who created me and has my best interests at the heart of His plan for me?

Jeremiah 29:11 came alive to me that summer and assured me that God was weaving every experience of my life into His incredible plan, not to devastate me but rather to be an integral part of the hope and future He designed for my life. This was just the beginning of God getting hold of my heart and setting it on fire with the dreams and plans He had for me.

"For I know the plans I have for you," declares the Lord, "plans to prosper you and not to harm you, plans to give you a hope and a future."

—Jeremiah 29:11

ONE DEFINING DREAM

As that pivotal summer at camp continued, I grew so much in my relationship with God and through the opportunities to sing at each meeting. God had done so much for me that I could hardly wait to get up each day and sing for Him.

However, one day everything changed. After I got done singing my songs, I began to find my way to my seat but was stopped dead in my tracks as the director very spontaneously asked me to come back up on stage to share my story. While this may not seem like a big deal to some, it was a huge deal to me. I had never shared the story of my past and certainly didn't want to start in front of several hundred of my peers. I didn't want them to know that I didn't have a perfect life.

I froze and didn't know what to do. My mind quickly raced through the following options: I could sprint out the back door, but that would make a scene; I could try to politely decline, but I could sense he wasn't going to take no for an answer; last, I could try to gracefully trudge through it and hope for the best. I chose the latter of the three, took a deep breath, and started in.

Much to my horror, talking about my childhood was messy, and exactly what I feared would happen did happen. I completely fell apart. Now, I'm not talking about the graceful tear rolling down my cheek as I eloquently shared from the depths of my soul. No, it was more like an avalanche of snot coming out of my nose as I stammered and barely choked out my words. I was absolutely mortified and wanted just to close my eyes, click my heels together like Dorothy, and instantly vanish!

Somehow, I pulled myself together and made my way back to my seat, wishing that moment would be forgotten, all the while knowing it was one of those undeniably awkward moments that would be permanently etched in everyone's minds. Despite my complete mortification, God did something that week that changed me forever.

Throughout the week, about fifty of the teenagers came up to me at different times and wanted to talk. One girl shared that her mom and dad had just divorced and she was really struggling. A boy shared of his personal struggle with drugs and alcohol. Another girl showed me on her wrist where she had tried to take her life. On and on the stories went—stories of hurt, stories of rejection, and stories of broken hearts and shattered dreams.

For the first time in my life, I realized that everything I had experienced happened for a reason. Nothing was by mistake or coincidence. All had prepared me for this very moment in time when I could relate to each of these precious teenagers. No, I didn't have any big, profound answers, but I could look them in the eyes and say, "Yes, I know what it is like to hurt, but I also know what it is like to have a God who is faithful and who has been with me every step of the way. And all I know is that this same God loves you too and will be faithful to you as well."

By the end of the week, I knew without a doubt that God had literally changed my hopes and dreams. As much as I loved music, God had a different plan for me. He wanted to use the story of His faithfulness in my life to make a difference in the lives of others.

THE GOOD, BAD & UGLY

I think so many times we want to offer God the good things we have—our talents, our abilities, and the things we like and are proud of, but God wants everything. He wants the good, the bad, the ugly, the embarrassing, and then He wants to turn it around and make something beautiful out of it to use for His glory and His Kingdom. Isaiah 61:3 talks about beauty coming from our ashes. You might wonder, *How could anything beautiful come from the ashes of past failures and heartaches in life?* But I assure you that this is truly what God specializes in, for there is nothing in our lives that God can't turn around and restore to bring the greatest glory to His name.

Not only does God bring beauty from our ashes, but He also gives strength in our weakness (2 Cor. 12:9). We all face moments when we feel weak and perhaps even unable to put one foot in front of the other to live out our dreams, but when we intimately know Jesus, He can fill those weak places in our hearts with His power and His strength. It blows my mind that the same power that raised Jesus from the dead is available to you and to me. If we will just grab on to His power each day, there is no telling what He can and will do in and through us as we live out the dreams He has placed within our hearts.

PURPOSE IN OUR PAIN

Here's the thing that I am most excited to share with you: when we cling to God's power and choose to use *everything* in our lives for His glory, that is when the healing begins in our own lives. We begin to see opportunities before us instead of focusing on past failures and disappointments that are behind us. We recognize chances to use our experiences, good or bad, as a way to help others, and, in doing so, we may begin to invest our lives in making a difference for the Kingdom. Before long, the pain is quietly replaced with the excitement of knowing there is purpose for our pain and fulfillment in being used by God for His life-changing and eternal purposes.

Maybe your picket fence is no longer white and maybe it's tattered and falling apart. My prayer as we journey through this book together is that maybe, just maybe, you will find the courage to pick up the pieces of your fence and begin to dream again. Yes, life is still hard and dreams aren't always easily accomplished, but I promise you, if you lay it all on the line, God will come through and prove Himself faithful every time.

Take it from a girl who started out without any hope or any future but found there was a God who reached down in His love and literally saved and rescued me. Because of the miraculous work He did in my life, I can't help but share and spur you on to the dreams He is speaking into your life. It is what you were chosen and created for.

So, let's dig in and explore God's amazing dreams. Oh, and by the way, maybe I am that Christian cheerleader I dreamed of as a child, and perhaps you are exactly who God had in mind for me to cheer on. As we embark on this journey together, I want you to know that I am cheering for you, believing in you, and praying for you as you discover the awesome purposes and dreams God has for you!

Dream Weaving

Everyone longs to have a perfect story. You know, the one that begins with "Once upon a time" and ends with "happily ever after." But those stories are aptly called "fairy tales," and they are not the stories of our lives. Our stories are stories of real people wrestling through the joys and struggles of real life. And what we do with our struggles and our stories makes all the difference in the world.

What were your dreams as a child and even as an adult?

_____

_____

_____

_____

_____

_____

What has stood in the way of your living out those dreams?

_____

_____

_____

_____

_____

_____

_____

_____

_____

Can you think back to a time when you surrendered all your hopes, dreams, and your future to God? If so, take a few moments to journal about that defining decision in your life.

_____

_____

_____

_____

_____

_____

_____

_____

_____

_____

_____

_____

_____

_____

Take a moment and write a prayer to the Creator of the dreams of your heart and soul. Ask Him to breathe into your life a fresh word and anointing. Make a commitment to dedicate your all to fulfilling His purpose to bring the greatest glory to His name.

_____

_____

_____

_____

_____

_____

_____

_____

_____

_____

_____

_____

_____

Chapter 2

A Visit with Destiny

MY STORY BEGINS ON A COOL OCTOBER DAY.

The chilly autumn air gave ominous warning to the harsh New England winter that would soon follow. But perhaps the ominous warning was not just felt in the air but within the heart of a woman packing her three small children and all her belongings into her car to begin a long trip to a new beginning. It was a trip that evoked fear and uncertainty as she moved to be near a husband who was states away serving a prison sentence.

With every mile she drove, her mind raced with questions and doubts about her future. What if this didn't work out? How would she ever raise three babies on her own? Their relationship was rocky at best from the start. Both had come from previous marriages with tons of baggage. What ever made her feel this would be different?

Yet, with all the ups and downs, he was her heart and her life and the father to these three beautiful children ages four, two, and the littlest one being only a few weeks old. She mustered all the courage and resolve that she could and determinedly set out for her new life with the hope of a fresh start for all of them.

The days were hectic as she settled in and unpacked while also caring for the demands of three small children. Soon the unpacking was finished, however, and loneliness set in like a heavy fog obscuring the view of her hopeful horizons of happiness. By the end of each long and difficult day, the weary mom would collapse in her bed exhausted and alone. The busyness of the day kept her mind occupied and distracted her from going to the dark places, but at night the depressing thoughts would torment her and rob her of the rest she so desperately needed. She could feel herself slipping into a place that she didn't want to go.

Eventually, she knew she needed help. Something wasn't right within her, and she needed some answers. She remembered the doctor asking her to come back for a checkup as soon as possible after delivering her last baby. But, with the move and all the chaos, this detail was forgotten until now.

Desperate for answers, she packed up the children and bravely went to see a physician. Nothing prepared her for what she would hear. It was the word she secretly feared and the word that would further diminish her hopes and dreams.

Cancer.

Grappling with the reality of the disease, she barely heard anything else the doctor said. She gathered her babies and stumbled to her car and drove home in shock as if in a trance of disbelief. What would she do now? How would she take care of these children, especially the baby?

In the ensuing days, this brave woman constantly battled the onslaught of worry and tears, but before long it became difficult to even get out of bed and take care of herself, let alone her children. It was on one of those desolate days, however, that the doorbell rang and a divine appointment changed everything.

Just a few miles away from this desperate mom and her three small children was a couple that had experienced the transforming power of Jesus in their lives. They too had a rocky marriage in their past, plagued with fighting and drinking, but they had miraculously and radically been changed through a personal relationship with Jesus.

With overflowing hearts of gratitude for God's work in their lives, this couple couldn't help but share with as many people as possible the hope in Christ that had changed them so completely. They understood that God could use even their past to make a difference in someone's life. So, each week they would randomly choose houses and neighborhoods and go door-to-door sharing about Jesus and inviting people to church. It was on one of these random neighborhood visits that their lives intersected with this family in need.

It was no mistake or coincidence that they chose this house that day. God sent them, and this visit forever impacted the lives of all involved.

With their Bibles in hand, the couple from the church quickly walked up the stairs with excitement and rang the doorbell, anxious to share about Jesus and invite people to their church. They were in no way prepared for what they found. A little girl answered the door of the dimly-lit house, and moments later they witnessed the grim reality of a sick and bedridden mom surrounded by a four-year-old, two-year-old, and a six-week-old baby.

The couple's gleeful invitation to visit their church was stuck in their throats. The urgency of the situation beckoned them to step into this woman's life and offer her a lifeline. They knew they were stepping out on a limb because this woman didn't even know them. Who shows up as a stranger at a woman's house and offers to take her babies? As crazy as it sounded, they knew it was what they were supposed to do. There was no way they could turn their backs on such a desperate situation.

So, with compassion in their eyes, this heaven-sent couple boldly offered to help this mom by taking care of the children until she got better. The poor mom lay there devastated that it had come to this, complete strangers offering to take care of her babies. She knew she needed the help, but her heart just couldn't let them all go. These strangers had such kind eyes and such generous hearts though; it was almost like she had known them all along. Perhaps this was more than a random visit. *Maybe some sort of destiny...maybe some sort of miracle*, she mused.

Reluctantly, the mom agreed to let them take and care for the baby until she got better. Forcing herself out of bed, she and the strangers gathered what few belongings there were for the infant, and then she watched as the kind strangers left with her baby girl in their arms. Her heart was breaking, yet all the while she found some relief in knowing somebody cared enough to stop by and cared enough to get involved in her tragic story.

The days turned into weeks and the weeks turned into months as the family from the church continued to offer a helping hand. They would visit the baby's mom regularly to give her time with her baby and to help out with the other children. Eventually, the day the mom had been waiting for arrived: her husband came home from prison. Despite her illness, she had been dreaming of this day for months. She hoped for a better life with him and her children and just knew it would be different this time. However, those dreams were soon shattered as things seemed to pick up right where they left off, with the drinking that led to more fighting, and the vicious cycle continued. This time it was much worse; in addition to fighting for a marriage that was falling apart, she was also fighting for her life. The cancer had initially responded to the treatments and even went into remission for a few years, but the remission was short-lived. The cancer eventually came back with a vengeance and gradually ravaged her entire body.

Throughout all of these turbulent years, the couple from the church stood by this family and helped in any way they could. Their hearts were repeatedly broken as the baby they so lovingly cared for bounced back and forth between both families. Yet, despite the emotional roller coaster they were often on, this family following God's mission always reached out and showed love to the hurting mother and her children—a decision prompted by the heart of God and a decision carried straight to the heart of God.

As the end drew near, the mom took her last breath and quietly slipped far away from the pain in her body and far from the pain in her heart. Life never got easier for her. There was no Prince Charming who whisked her away in her dreams, and there was no happy ending. Instead, the cruel reality of one disappointment after another slowly chiseled a hole in her heart so deep that it was only God Himself who could carry her through the darkest moments. She had accepted Jesus into her life on one of the visits with the couple from the church, and thereafter, even in the midst of her heartache and pain, she knew beyond a shadow of a doubt that God loved her and was with her and that she would spend eternity with Him in Heaven where there would be no tears, no pain, and no suffering. It was that hope and that peace that she clung to until her dying day.

Not too long after the mom's death, both the older daughter and son, when they each turned fourteen, were kicked out of the house and forced to face life alone. Rejection, hurt, and pain all passed down to their innocent hearts. The cycle never breaking. The pain never ending.

The youngest daughter, after her mom died, lived with the family from the church permanently since the dad didn't care either way. From that point on, she knew she had a family that loved her, and she knew that she would always have a place to call home.

You may have figured it out by now, but I was that six-week-old baby girl. I was the one Jesus rescued out of a very destitute situation and whose life was radically changed. I often ask, *Why me? Why did I get chosen? What if this couple had not come to my house that day? Or what if they had just dropped off literature about their church and went on their merry way?* My life would have been so different. My story would not be the same. This couple's faithfulness to God and their willingness to follow the dreams He placed before them led them to my house that day, that day that was ordained by God before the very foundations of the earth. And their decision to bring Jesus to my house literally changed the course of my life forever.

I don't have all the answers to my questions, but this I know: There are no mistakes with God. He will use everything, including our pain, for His purposes. He is the author of my story, a story that shows how He loved me, He chose me, He rescued me, He saved me, and now He is using me more than I could ever imagine possible and taking me beyond my wildest dreams every time I am privileged to stand in front of audiences to sing and share from my heart.

I know beyond a shadow of a doubt that it is only because of God's work in my life and in my story that I am able to live out the dreams He has breathed into my heart. The story of my life has become the passion of my heart—using what I have been through to show hurting people that there is hope in Jesus! That's my story. That's my dream. What's yours?

Dream Weaving

Everyone has a story, and our stories are an intricate part of the purpose and the dreams for our lives. While each story may be similar in some ways, they are all unique and imprinted by the sovereign hand of God. When we see Him at work weaving our story into the fabric of His plan for our lives, we can find great comfort, peace, and fulfillment in knowing that the God of the universe loves us and cares about every single detail of our lives. Nothing goes undetected and nothing escapes His heart. Every part of our story becomes part of our purpose when we allow God to write the dreams of our lives.

What's the story of your life? Take a moment to reflect and write about a few monumental moments when God showed up and worked in your life, crafting a story that could only be from Him.

_____

_____

_____

_____

_____

_____

_____

_____

_____

_____

_____

_____

_____

_____

How do you see God weaving your story into the dreams and purpose of your life?

_____

_____

_____

_____

_____

_____

_____

_____

_____

_____

_____

_____

_____

_____

_____

_____

Have you ever shared parts of your story to encourage or inspire others? Think of some ways you could do so this week.

_____

_____

_____

_____

_____

_____

_____

_____

_____

_____

_____

_____

_____

Have you ever thought that God may want to use you to literally change the course of someone's life? Don't worry! That doesn't mean you have to take a baby home, but what it could mean is that, by being intentional, you could impact the eternity of one whom God brings into your life. Ask the Lord to open your eyes and your heart to the opportunities around you, and then be ready to get involved. Not only will the lives of others be changed, but yours will never be the same as well!

_____

_____

_____

_____

_____

_____

_____

_____

_____

_____

_____

Chapter 3

Stepping on the Clouds

The journey ahead is awesome. But you can't get started until you've developed a dream.

—John Maxwell

DREAMS ARE ESSENTIAL TO EVERY ONE OF US. Whether hidden or acknowledged, tucked away or lived out, in the secret places of our hearts we all have the potential to form dreams that give our lives the meaning and fulfillment we all desire.

A DREAM DEFINED

So, what exactly is a dream? I think sometimes we make it

more difficult and more lofty than it really is. We may even set ourselves up for failure by grabbing on to one all-consuming goal that we never quite attain, such as winning the Olympics, becoming President of the United States, starting a billion-dollar company, achieving a spot on the *New York Times* bestseller list, and on and on it goes. It's not that any of these examples are bad. In fact, they are all quite noble! I am all about being the best we can be, but the reality is that our dreams are defined when we catch a glimpse of how God can use us as we make ourselves available to Him. That's it. Living our dreams is simply living out the purposes for which God created us!

Our dreams are defined when we catch a glimpse of how God can use us as we make ourselves available to Him.

The Bible is full of examples of ordinary people who caught a glimpse of what God could do through them, who rose to the occasion to live out those purposes, and who literally changed the world. Joseph was one such example. At seventeen years old, he was a bright boy who was gifted in interpreting dreams. However, this gift ignited a flame of resentment in his older brothers. They despised him and conspired to sell him into slavery. Oh, the betrayal Joseph must have felt when he was dragged away to Egypt, far away from his family and far away from the life he knew.

Despite the betrayal from his family, God was with Joseph and placed him with Potiphar, a successful captain of the guard in Pharaoh's army. Joseph quickly found favor in Potiphar's household and was in charge of all that Potiphar owned. Life had turned around for him as he used his talents and gifts in the opportunities set before him. But it was not long before he faced another setback.

Potiphar's wife became attracted to Joseph, made advances toward him, and was denied by him. In her humiliation, and to cover her actions, she went to Potiphar and made false accusations that Joseph had made the advances. Potiphar was furious and immediately had Joseph thrown into prison. Once again Joseph, hurt and betrayed, found himself a victim of someone else's wrongdoing.

A DREAM CONFINED

I'm sure there were days in that prison when he fought off the constant foes of bitterness, anger, and hurt. I'm sure there were days when he wanted to give up. Somehow Joseph hung on and woke up ready to give his all each day, ready to do the next thing that was before him. It was on one of those menial days when doing the "next thing" propelled him from the prison to the palace.

Pharaoh had a dream that troubled him immensely. He told all of his wise men and those closest to him, but no one could come up with any answers, that is until Pharaoh's cupbearer just happened to remember Joseph interpreting one of his dreams two years prior (while he was briefly in prison with Joseph). They quickly summoned Joseph to hear Pharaoh's dream, and Joseph accurately and thoroughly described the dream and its meaning. The interpretation was both a warning of an upcoming famine as well as a plan of action to prepare for and survive it. Pharaoh was amazed and impressed by Joseph's abilities and by the God within him. He immediately put him in charge of his house and his kingdom. Next to Pharaoh himself, there was no one greater.

A DREAM RESTORED

At thirty years old, Joseph had risen from a pit of despair to a pinnacle of prosperity. God had strategically placed Joseph as head over Egypt to prepare for this seven-year famine that would impact the world. People came from all over trying to buy food to survive. And I believe the grandiose moment where Joseph's story collided with God's destiny for him was the moment his family showed up to buy grain. That seventeen-year-old dreamer despised by his brothers would now be the hand that fed them. That hole in his heart would now be filled by this reunion with his father and a fresh start with his brothers.

Everything in Joseph's life played a part and led up to the climax of this story. It wasn't that Joseph aggressively pursued this lofty dream to become the head of Egypt. It was that Joseph was faithful in the small things and diligent each day. It was rising above his circumstances when everything in him screamed defeat. It was letting go of the past and looking forward to his future. It was choosing not to live in bitterness but rather turning it around and using what he had been through for good. All of this prepared him and propelled him to the center of God's dream and God's plan for his life.

Maybe you can relate to the hurt and betrayal that Joseph experienced. Perhaps you also know what it is like to be a victim of unfair circumstances. Joseph's life is such a great reminder to all of us that our circumstances do not have to define us or determine our future. From his example, we can see that it is possible to rise above the pain of the past to experience the possibilities of the future. The choice is up to us.

You might be wondering where to begin to be faithful in your own life as Joseph was in his. "That's a great story," you might say, "but how do I know what God has for me?" The fact that you are reading this book is a great indication that you are ready to find and pursue the dreams God has for you. So, let's take a look at a few practical steps to figuring out what those dreams are.

SEEK GOD

The first step in finding God's dreams for your life is to wake up each day and start right where you are. Whatever God places right before you and leads you to do, give it your all. I like to start my day off by asking God to direct me into what He wants me to do because, left to myself, I can stay busy without ever really landing on what's important and significant.

A man's heart plans his way, but the Lord determines his steps.
—*Proverbs 16:9 NKJV*

If we seek God right at the start of our day, asking Him to lead and guide us, I believe He will determine our steps just as He did for Joseph. It was no mistake that the cupbearer was in prison with Joseph. It was no mistake that that same cupbearer ended up working for Pharaoh and recommended Joseph to interpret the dream. God orchestrated all the details and all the steps to bring Joseph into His incredible plan, and God will do the same in our lives if we are seeking Him each day.

Years ago, my husband and I were offered jobs as directors of a Christian camp on the West Coast. With this opportunity, we were offered wonderful salaries and weekends off to allow me the opportunity to continue singing with my ministry. It definitely seemed like an offer we couldn't refuse, yet the more we prayed and sought God's face about it, the less peace we had moving forward with it. Finally, when the time came for us to give a definite answer, after diligently bathing this amazing opportunity in prayer, we had to decline. In some ways, we felt crazy for doing so, but we knew in our hearts that God was not directing our steps forward with it.

Then, not even a year later, we were sad to hear that the camp had gone through hard times and had to shut its doors. I can't even begin to tell you the relief we felt in knowing that God protected us from packing everything up and moving across the country only to find that it was not going to work out. We learned in a powerful way the importance of God determining our steps rather than us determining our own, and we learned that this can only be done when we are seeking God diligently each day.

Interestingly, it wasn't too long after we turned down the camp opportunity that God opened some major doors of opportunity for both of us that completely aligned with our dreams and goals. Once again, we were reminded that God always knows what is best for us and will reveal His plan to us if we are seeking Him.

WELCOME CHANGE

Another way to discover our dreams would be to try new things and to be willing to step out of our comfort zones. However, if you are anything like me, then change is difficult. I have friends who, on the other hand, love change. In fact, I have several friends who break open a can of paint when they are bored and are able to transform a room in a matter of hours. I have other friends who change the arrangement of their furniture frequently, sometimes on a weekly basis. These things make me break out in hives just thinking about them. I figure once my house is set up I'm good until we either move or die! And then there's my hair. I would probably wear the same hairstyle to the grave if it weren't for my wonderful hairdresser pushing me at times to change things up.

As silly as those examples may be, I have to wonder if sometimes that's what we do in other areas of our lives. We get so terrified of change that we stay stuck doing the same things over and over and possibly miss out on some of the greatest opportunities God has for us. Always living in our comfort zones does not usually equate to living out our dreams. We were created for more than just being comfortable; we were created to make a difference.

Always living in our comfort zones does not usually equate to living out our dreams.

Stepping out of our comfort zones and fully depending on God is what launches us into the sweet spot of the center of His dreams for our lives. It also forces dependence on God rather than ourselves. When we step out of what we are comfortable with and trust God for what He can do, He shows up and performs the miraculous. We can find great encouragement in knowing that God is able to do far beyond what we could ever imagine.

We can be courageous in stepping out because it isn't about what we can or can't do; it is all about God and what He *will* do when we make ourselves available to Him.

Now to Him who is able to do exceedingly abundantly above all that we ask or think, according to the power that works in us.
—*Ephesians 3:20* NKJV

BE BOLD

Children are so fun to watch. Many times they will boldly walk around not letting anything stand in the way of their sought-after goal. Perhaps we should take a lesson from them.

I remember as a young person going to Vacation Bible School each summer. One particular year the church had a contest. Whoever brought the most visitors to Bible School would win a 10-speed bike. I didn't have a bike, and I just knew this was going to be the way I would get one. So, I began inviting anyone and everyone who looked the right age to go to VBS with me.

As I went door-to-door inviting kids, I would carefully write down all their information so that I could follow-up on who was coming and who needed rides. The rule was that adults could not do the inviting but could help with transporting the children. The night before Bible School started, I began calling all of my prospects. To make a long story short, my family had to rent a school bus because I brought seventy-two kids with me on the first day of VBS.

My husband relentlessly teases me by saying, "Paula, you are such an overachiever. Second place only had five. You couldn't have just brought ten kids and called it good. No, you had to make sure no one even came close."

Then in college I even received a letter from the National Board of Vacation Bible School telling me that I still held the national record of most visitors brought to Bible School. Okay, so I am an overachiever. And I know it's a crazy story, but here's the deal: I believed back then and I still believe today that we have a BIG God who can do BIG things in and through us—not just five-person things but seventy-two person things! If we will just have the faith and boldness of a child, then the sky is truly the limit in what God can accomplish!

CREATE WHITE SPACE

Carving out time to dream is another important aspect of discovering the dreams God has for us. So often we have ourselves on tight schedules with no margin and no white space to focus our thoughts to even think through our days, much less our dreams and goals.

I admit it! I can be the queen of trying to stuff way more into twenty-four hours than what is even humanly possible. Perhaps a recent less-than-stellar morning showcases this best. It began the moment my eyes popped open and I dashed out of bed and rushed downstairs for a few quiet moments of reading my Bible and guzzling a cup or two of coffee before I dove headfirst into my day. After lingering for a few-too-many extra moments to finish writing out the day's endless to-do list, I began racing around at breakneck speed getting Emma and myself ready, making all the beds and throwing in some laundry, emptying the dishwasher, and only leaving a few frenzied moments (that I call "crunch time") for packing Emma's lunch and backpack, grabbing her spelling words, and making a mad dash to the car all the while fielding questions of, "What should I take for show-and-tell?," "When are you coming to lunch, mommy?," and "What are we doing after school?"

By the time I regrouped and caught my breath in the car, we were in the thick of the morning rush-hour commute, a drive that involved careful attention to the cars weaving in and out of traffic around me but also involved addition and subtraction quizzing, reviewing spelling words, and rehearsing songs for the upcoming church Christmas program. We arrived at school fifteen minutes early with most of my morning tasks checked off, but all of the chaos and all of the frenzy left me feeling like all I had accomplished was a whirlwind of anxiety.

I know we can all have crazy mornings, but I have found that if I am not careful, noise, adrenaline, and non-stop activity can become the mainstay of my entire day. Without realizing it, I can constantly live in "crunch time" mode, which only leads to frustration, stress, and my becoming not a very fun person to be around.

This is where intentionally making time to shut out the noise of life to think through and plan our days, to catch our breaths, and to dream is imperative in this fast-paced world we all live in. Simply stated, carving out white space involves preparing for the details of today while also planning our dreams for tomorrow. Whether it's going on a walk in nature to clear our heads or curling up with a journal and a cup of tea to write out our hopes and dreams, taking time each day to create a few moments of white space is so healthy and necessary. It steadies our minds and soothes our souls, making us better able to juggle our responsibilities and live out our dreams.

DO WHAT YOU ENJOY

Last, and perhaps most important, we need to figure out what we enjoy and then explore ways to use it to make a difference in this world. I think sometimes we worry that getting serious about living out God's dreams means He will make us do something we don't enjoy. But the One who created us actually factored our talents, our likes, and our dislikes into His master plan! Perhaps He even designed us with all of those specific interests and abilities for a reason.

I love to see people using what they enjoy doing to help others. I shared about singing at that Christian camp when I was fourteen. Well, when the camp called and invited me to come for the summer, I asked my family if I could go. They responded by saying they needed to pray about it, so I gave them a night to do so, and the next morning they said, "You can go to camp, but we are going with you." So, we all packed up and headed to teen camp for the entire summer.

I was the only teenager who brought adults to camp. Dad

worked hard each day on maintenance—fixing leaky toilets, repairing cabin roofs, and tending to a host of other issues that needed attention in order for the camp to run properly. Mom, on the other hand, bounced out of bed at 4:30 each morning and headed to the kitchen to get homemade dough rising for cinnamon rolls that would go with the scrambled eggs, bacon, oatmeal, and freshly-cut fruit.

No sooner was breakfast over and cleaned up before it was on to preparing yet another made-from-scratch meal complete with mouth-watering desserts. After lunch came and went, it was on to dinner, which on any given night consisted of food that kids would rave about for weeks to follow. In fact, many of these kids had never eaten anything homemade, and by the end of the week many didn't want to leave.

But I want you to know my family's faithful work each day was so much more than just fixing faucets and cooking meals. It was ALL about taking what they enjoyed and allowing God to use it for His Kingdom. You see, there is no doubt in my mind that every act of service they rendered played a part in creating an environment where decisions for Christ were made every week, and there was no greater joy within their hearts than being a part of something so much bigger than themselves, something eternal.

LIVE BEYOND YOURSELF

I met Miss Rose a few years ago in Gladstone, Oregon, at a

conference where I was speaking. All weekend long I had passionately shared about living out God's dreams. To my surprise, this sweet, eighty-year-old lady came up to me at the end of the weekend excited to share what God had breathed into her heart.

Miss Rose had always felt called into missions. For various reasons, she never was able to fulfill that dream. However, God was not finished with Miss Rose, and all throughout the weekend He stirred her heart and reignited this dream of long ago. She beamed with joy and couldn't get her words out fast enough as she told me all in one breath that her church was going to be taking a mission trip and she had decided to sign up and go. Surely she could help the missionaries in some way.

I couldn't help but picture this amazing, eighty-year-old woman boarding a plane and heading to a faraway land to fulfill her lifelong dream of sharing Jesus with the lost! I could hardly contain my excitement because that is what it is all about— catching a glimpse of how God can use us as we make ourselves available to Him. It doesn't matter how old or how young we may be. If we are willing and available, God will use us to accomplish His dreams and His purposes for our lives!

So, when was the last time you took a leap of faith toward your dream? Maybe it involves beginning, changing, or ending a career. Maybe you need to pursue mending a relationship or following through on a commitment. Maybe His still, small voice is calling you to get involved in ministry.

Only you can search your heart to discover God's plan and

His dreams for you. But one thing I do know for myself is that I don't want to look back in thirty years and wish I had done things differently. I don't want to just go through life surviving, coping, and existing. I want more than that. I want the abundant life that Jesus talks about in John 10:10, a life that I believe is found when we are seeking Him and boldly chasing after the dreams He has placed within our hearts. Whether it's preparing meals at a camp for teens or jumping on a plane to minister to people in need, God will use us beyond what we could ever imagine to make a difference far beyond our wildest dreams.

Dream Weaving

Living out our dreams is simply catching a glimpse of how God can use us as we make ourselves available to Him. We can find how He wants to use us when we boldly seek His face each day. How exciting it is to know that the God of the universe uniquely made each of us and will use all of our experiences, our talents, and even what we enjoy for His glory. He loves to take us beyond ourselves to use us for that which is life-changing and eternal.

What steps are you currently taking toward your dream?

_____

_____

_____

_____

_____

_____

Is there anything outside of your comfort zone that you are avoiding? If so, what is it?

_____

_____

_____

_____

_____

_____

_____

_____

What is something you would go after if you were bold and fearless like a child?

_____

_____

_____

_____

_____

What do you enjoy doing that could potentially be a part of your dream? Be creative and think of ways your interests could tie into your dream and purpose.

_____

_____

_____

_____

_____

_____

_____

_____

_____

Take a few moments and write out a prayer asking God to show you this week how to proceed from here in living out the dreams He has for you.

_____

_____

_____

_____

_____

_____

_____

_____

_____

_____

_____

_____

_____

_____

_____

_____

_____

Chapter 4

Scaling the Mountains

AT SOME POINT, WE ALL COME TO A CROSSROADS IN life where we must decide how far we will go and what price we will pay to live out the dreams God has for us. Achieving our dreams takes hard work for the long haul. We have to consider the costs and the obstacles to overcome as we traverse this winding journey of living in the center of God's dreams.

A few months ago, to my husband's sheer delight, we were invited to attend a private dinner at the Smithsonian National Air and Space Museum in Washington, D.C. He was like a kid in a candy store, savoring every moment of seeing his favorite aircrafts up close and personal. For me, what was most impressive was the IMAX movie they showed us that night. The movie was a documentary about a group of hikers embarking on one of the greatest challenges known to mankind: Mount Everest. I watched with sheer amazement and, at times, horror as we were given an inside look at what the journey entailed.

At 29, 029 feet above sea level, Everest embodies the breathtaking thrill of victory or the devastating agony of defeat to each person who bravely seeks its conquest. The documentary painted a picture of the difficulties the climbers faced each day as they tried to realize their dream. The reality is that, while all started out determined and committed to the end, not everyone made it to the top on this particular voyage. Despite their meticulous preparations, treacherous weather conditions and unforeseen problems continuously attacked each climber's resolve. It was a battle that intensified with each step, a battle that David Breashears, the leader of the group, knew all too well. And, as a storm came out of nowhere, he was left for dead by the others. Nearly blind and with his hands close to being frozen completely, he was in desperate shape yet somehow dug from deep within and kept walking.[1]

Beck Weathers, another hiker in the group, gives the following testament to his experience on that fateful day:

> All I knew was that, as long as my legs would run and I could stand up, I was gonna move toward that camp. And if I fell down, I was gonna get up. And if I fell down again, I was gonna get up. And I was gonna keep movin' till I either hit that camp or walked off the face of that mountain.[2]

These men somehow found the resolve and pushed through

the pain, took the risk, and gave it their all with nothing held back. They were either going to succeed or die trying. The last stretch nearly did them in as they reached such high altitude levels that they could barely move, let alone breathe, even with oxygen devices. Still, their unwavering commitment and undaunted persistence paid off as they gloriously reached the summit. In that one moment, it didn't matter what the journey looked like because they survived and reached their lifelong goal of conquering the highest mountain in the world.

Was it the breathtaking view and the picturesque sky that made their trek worthwhile? No, I believe it was much more than that. I believe in the end they celebrated the strength that they found in digging deeper and moving forward despite all the odds that were against them. It was also the mindset that giving up would never be an option that carried them through the days when doubt was knocking on their heart's doors. Oh, I can see them all today sitting around a campfire with their families, telling their tale—a tale not just about the mountaintop; no, what will forever captivate their listeners will be the story of their journey.

VISION BEYOND OUR CIRCUMSTANCES

While I doubt many of us will take on the challenge of Mount Everest in a literal sense, we do face mountains of our own throughout life. Mountains that stand between us and our dreams. Mountains that must be overcome with that same tenacity and resolve as the climbers of Everest. Part of facing the mountains in our lives is having vision to see past the present circumstances and having the fortitude to do whatever it takes to stick it out. It all begins with vision.

Vision is seeing above what looks impossible, not accepting the status quo, and living many times beyond where the majority set up camp. The Bible shows us the importance of vision in Proverbs 29:18 [KJV]: "Where there is no vision, the people perish."

All of us were created with a purpose. Unfortunately, not everyone finds that purpose because it takes commitment, discipline, endurance, and hard work to find the vision God has for our lives. People who do find their purpose and successfully live in it are the ones who do not look for the easy way out. They are usually characterized by their tenacious spirits and by their willingness to sacrifice convenience for what's necessary.

Jesus had something to say about taking the easy road. He tells us in Luke 9:23 that whoever wants to be His disciple must deny themselves and take up their cross daily and follow Him.

Now, our cross will never be what His cross was, but it may involve sticking it out when we would rather give up, working hard without the appreciation we so desire, and rising above the obstacles that stand in our way. All of these examples go against our human nature, but all are where the rubber meets the road and where our vision and commitment are put to the test. The path to reaching our dreams is not designed with shortcuts. We must be willing to overcome all the obstacles that hold us back, and we must work hard and never take the easy way out.

Whether we scale the mountain of achieving our dreams or have the tendency to back down in defeat when it's not easy, it all comes down to our vision. Vision is what keeps us going when our dreams seem out of reach. Vision keeps us focused and motivated when the odds are stacked against us. And vision is the driving force that takes us beyond where we are to get us where we want to be. I know life can be hard, and sometimes we can feel so battered and worn out that taking steps toward our dreams can feel impossible. It's important to realize that just because God puts a dream within our hearts doesn't mean it will be easy to achieve. However, what it does mean is that God is with us, and if we will have the vision to see beyond our circumstances and the fierce determination to see our dreams through, God will take us beyond our wildest dreams.

VISION BEYOND THE ODDS

Perhaps one of the greatest examples of "against all odds" vision is in Numbers 13 when Moses sent twelve scouts to check out the land in Canaan. Let me point out that Canaan was a land that was already promised by God to the Israelites, so this should have been a slam-dunk "Mount Everest" experience for them.

As Moses anxiously awaited the spies' return, I'm sure he dreamed and planned for the much-anticipated day of acquiring God's Promised Land. At the first glimpse of them on the horizon, Moses gathered the entire community eager to hear the good report of what they had found. The spies began by telling of the milk and honey that flowed freely in the Land of Canaan just as they had always dreamed of. They brought clusters of grapes, pomegranates, and figs to show the bountiful fruit that filled the land.

Imagine the cheers and the excitement of the crowd. That is, until ten of the spies began to share what they really thought and chose to see their circumstances as impossible rather than resting in the promises of God.

The ten spies reported that the Canaanites were strong and the cities were large and fortified. They only saw impenetrable walls, not a land of milk and honey that was promised to them. Instead of scaling the mountain of God's Promised Land, they lost their vision and quickly retreated to what was safe and comfortable. It didn't take long for the pessimism of the spies to spread and contaminate the whole community.

The people wept and cried out to God asking why He had brought them to this land to die. How quickly they forgot that this same God had brought them out of Egypt, parted the Red Sea, provided manna from Heaven to eat, and led them with a cloud by day and a pillar of fire by night. What more could He do to assure them that He would take care of them and give them the victory? The Israelites had lost their vision and their faith in God's promise to them.

As the scene continued to unfold, Moses and Aaron fell on their faces before God. Then, when things seemed insurmountable, Caleb and Joshua stood up and testified that God would help His people overcome the odds and be victorious in all that He had promised them. He would help them defy Canaan's strong men and conquer their fortified cities. However, it was to no avail. The people had made their decision and would not listen to the vision Caleb and Joshua cast of taking the land with God's help.

The story ends with the people losing their dream of entering the Promised Land. This Promised Land that they had spent their whole lives dreaming of, telling their children about, and preparing for had now been forfeited by allowing their vision and their faith in God's promises to crumble.

I believe we all have that same choice each day. Are we going to trust God to help us overcome the obstacles, or are we going to retreat in defeat? Two different choices with two different outcomes. I don't know about you, but I want to scale the mountains of my dreams. I don't want to back down and miss out on one thing that God has for me.

The future is awesome, but we must not lose sight of the vision or the promise that God will give us exactly what we need for every step of the journey. So, take a deep breath, and let's keep climbing!

COUNT THE COST

In addition to anchoring our vision, we must also count the cost in order to reach the summit of our dreams. We will often have to make sacrifices along the way.

At the end of that life-changing summer camp I attended,

I went home chalking it up to a wonderful experience and a chapter of my life I would never forget. Little did I know, it was just the beginning of something I would never have dreamed possible.

Once I got home, I started receiving phone calls from many of the youth groups all over New England and Canada that attended the camp throughout the summer. They were calling to inquire about having me do a concert and share my story at their churches. I remember thinking, *God, I am only fourteen years old. What am I supposed to share with a church full of people and with a pastor sitting on the front row?* But that is exactly what God wanted, somebody who didn't know what to do or how to do it but who was willing and available.

So, off I went each weekend, and the adventure of living out my dream became a reality. Before long I was booked almost every weekend sharing my faith, my music, and my story. God began to breathe within me a burden and a passion for those who were hurting and needed Jesus, and I truly saw each concert as a once-in-a-lifetime opportunity to share what God had done in my life. My heart would overflow with excitement as I saw countless teens and adults make decisions for Christ every weekend.

However, along with the excitement of doing my concerts, I also quickly learned that there were some sacrifices that I would have to make in order to live out my dreams—sacrifices such as keeping up with homework while traveling so much, not being available for some fun activities with friends on the weekends, and even dealing with some jealousy and ridicule from my peers. Being on the road so much also concerned people who talked to my parents about the childhood I was missing out on. But what they didn't understand was that any activity I gave up (football games, slumber parties, shopping excursions, etc.) and any ridicule that I encountered could not compare to the fulfillment and reward of being in the center of God's dreams for my life. The fact is, I hardly remember missing out on anything because the reward of seeing lives changed far outweighed any sacrifice I could make.

Maybe you have made sacrifices of your own to pursue your dreams and have also faced disapproval from others. Perhaps you have chosen to pursue your passion rather than climb the corporate ladder. Or maybe you have chosen to invest your time and money into a cause that you fiercely believe in rather than into a 401k.

Just this week, my husband and I attended a fundraiser for Freedom 4/24, a non-profit organization with a clear-cut mission to rescue women out of the sex-trafficking industry. One of the leaders shared that he left the law firm where he worked to take on a full-time position within this organization because he had no choice but to follow the passion of his heart to rescue these young girls. I'm sure this was a huge financial sacrifice for him, and maybe there were people who questioned his decision. But after listening to him speak from the depths of his heart, there was no doubt that he was so fulfilled by living out the mission God had for him.

You see, no matter the sacrifice we make in living out our dreams, the fulfillment we in turn receive makes the sacrifice seem small and insignificant. The joy of living out the dreams we were created for far surpasses any sacrifices we make along the way.

The joy of living out the dreams we were created for far surpasses any sacrifices we make along the way.

STAY THE COURSE

Living out our dreams requires continuous motivation and hard work that often no one else knows about. Staying the course can be one of the sacrifices we just talked about, but our motivation is what we focus on—it is the choice to get out of bed each morning and take the next step toward our dreams. For some, just getting out of bed can be half the battle. But, once that first forward action is accomplished, we are well on our way.

Staying motivated in the pursuit of those glimpses of God's work in our lives involves doing what we need to do rather than what we want to do, and this can be emotionally, physically, and spiritually exhausting. Winston Churchill once said, "Most significant contributions that have been made by society have been made by people who are tired."[3] Can you relate? It's important to realize that living God's dreams is not based on feelings, but rather it is based on choices and a commitment to give our all regardless of how we feel.

Living God's dreams is not based on feelings, but rather it is based on choices and a commitment to give our all regardless of how we feel.

Do you want to know if your purpose on Earth is finished? Here's the answer: If you are breathing, it's not! None of us are off the hook. It doesn't matter how young or how old you may be, God has a unique purpose for each of us. Remember Miss Rose who courageously pursued the exciting dreams that God had breathed within her heart? She was all in and saw ways that God could use her despite the fact that she was eighty years old!

What if we took that same approach to life as Miss Rose and committed ourselves to staying the course with the dreams God has for us until our final breath? I have a feeling we would be blown away by all the dreams God still has for us to fulfill. It's important to realize that our purpose is never complete until we leave this earth. So, while we are here, let's give it our all and not allow anything to hold us back from all the ways God can use us until we see Him face-to-face.

PRACTICE TUNNEL VISION

Perhaps one of the greatest costs I have encountered is the risk of standing alone, for I have found all along the way that there are people who make it their mission to shoot down the hopes and dreams of others. They themselves don't dare to dream, so they don't want anyone else to either. Maybe you know a few people like that as well.

When I think back to my college days, it was such an exciting time of life. It is where I met my husband, and it most certainly shaped and molded me into an adult. I reflect on my time at Liberty University in Lynchburg, Virginia, with such gratefulness for an awesome Christian college experience. While there, I had the incredible privilege to travel and sing with Light Ministries and then with the Sounds of Liberty, both scholarship teams that afforded me a place to sing and helped me pay my way through school. This was an answer to prayer because I didn't have the money for college and certainly didn't want my family to take on that burden after all that they had already done for me. As I mentioned previously, I also had been traveling each weekend throughout high school, so continuing with that in college was a dream come true.

After completing my undergraduate work, I went right into my Master's Degree in counseling, all the while still traveling with the Sounds of Liberty. Slowly, however, God began to stir in my heart a passion to continue sharing my story and music through the ministry He began when I was a teenager.

After praying about it for months and seeing God open doors for me to venture out with my own ministry again, I finally mustered up the courage to tell those around me. I was excited to share what God was doing in my heart and just knew my peers and professors would support me and cheer me on. While some did just that, there were many who did not. I remember some friends and even some professors and mentors in my life telling me that it would never work. *Singers are a dime a dozen, and it doesn't pay the bills. You will need to find something more realistic and not be such a dreamer.* These were just a few of the comments they would make.

Now, I'm sure most meant well and were truly trying to give me wise counsel. However, what they didn't understand was that God had breathed something into my heart. When He does this it doesn't matter how unrealistic it may appear because He is going to provide for every venture that He guides us into, just as He would have done (and eventually did) for the Israelites.

I'll be honest, I was very disappointed and let down, but I had a choice to make. I could either let other people determine my future by me allowing them to affect what I knew God was calling me to do, or I could learn to tune out the negativity and focus exclusively on what God thought and had planned for my life. I learned to practice tunnel vision, looking beyond the present negative circumstances and focusing exclusively on the dream.

When we put ourselves out there and passionately follow God's dreams, people are not always going to understand. Thus, it is imperative that we are firmly grounded in our purposes and our visions so we don't waver at the first sign of opposition. Instead, we determine to prove the naysayers wrong, not because of who we are, but because of who God is!

Determine to prove the naysayers wrong, not because of who we are, but because of who God is!

By the way, some of the people who didn't believe in what God was calling me to do back in college are some of the very people who now say, "Paula, we are so proud of you and just knew you could do it." Funny how that works, isn't it? All I can say is that I am so glad God believed in me even when others didn't and that He chose to use me regardless of the odds.

Perhaps you have people right now in your life who don't believe in you or in the dreams of your heart. I just want to encourage you in the fact that God loves you, wants the best for you, and will never give up on you! Regardless of what other people may say or do, God believes in you and has an incredible plan for your life, and nothing can ever change that.

RISE ABOVE YOUR INSECURITIES AND FEARS

Once we understand the costs of our dreams, it also is important to recognize the obstacles that can stand in our way and prohibit us from experiencing all that God has for us. Often, the biggest obstacles that can hinder us right at the start are feelings of insecurity and inadequacy.

Whether it's standing in line as a child in gym class hoping not to be the last one picked for the kickball team or as an adult anxiously awaiting a call for a much-needed job interview, there are times in our lives when we don't feel like we measure up or we feel unsure about our situations.

There are many reasons for our insecurities—childhood memories, put downs, abuse, disabilities, rejection, abandonment, and the list goes on. But just remember this word of wisdom from Eleanor Roosevelt: "No one can make you feel foolish or inferior without your permission." No matter what happens in our lives, we can choose how we will respond to our circumstances.

I remember worrying about a lot of things as a child. While many children only have to figure out what toy to play with each day, I was sometimes trying to figure out which family I would end up living with. I worried about people dying and leaving me alone and struggled with separation issues. I also found myself trying so hard to please everyone around me; yet, despite those gallant efforts, I often felt like I was disappointing someone.

My insecurities, worries, and perpetual people-pleasing continued into adulthood until I finally dealt with it by answering the following questions:

1. Who am I really living for?
2. Am I looking to find my security in God or in other people?

3. Am I more concerned with what people think or what God thinks?

I began to realize that we can never please everyone, but we can always please God when we put Him first and live wholeheartedly for Him.

Ultimately, we deal with our insecurities by recognizing that we can only become healthy and whole through Jesus. When we completely look to God alone to fill the wounded places of our hearts, we can find freedom from all of our insecurities and fears.

What insecurity is holding you back? I have learned that if you face your fears, you will conquer them; but, if you run from your fears, you will only increase them.

If you face your fears, you will conquer them; but, if you run from your fears, you will only increase them.

Last spring I was recording a new album for my ministry, which is always such an exciting venture. I feel so blessed to do what I love to do that sometimes I just have to pinch myself to make sure that it is real. As I record the albums, I am so privileged to have some of the very best musicians in Nashville on my projects. (Talk about feeling insecure and inadequate!) I often find myself wondering why I am even in the room with these amazing musicians. On one such day, I just so happened to take a bathroom break and saw a sign with a quote from John Wayne staring back at me. The quote read, "Courage is being scared to death but saddling up anyway." Wow, it was like God Himself hung that sign right there for me that day.

You see, we are all scared to death at times, even those of us who have been doing what we do for years. The key is pushing through our fears and anxiety by recognizing that we aren't in this alone. God is with us every step of the way and will give us exactly what we need to accomplish His purposes. He tells us in Philippians 4:13 that we can do *all* things through Christ who strengthens us. What would it look like if we really embraced and believed that verse? I believe we would let go of our fears and insecurities and we would saddle up for the exciting adventure God has waiting for us.

PICK YOURSELF UP

Success in life is going from one failure to another with undiminished enthusiasm.
—Winston Churchill

Imagine if we truly adopted that "undiminished enthusiasm" approach to our lives. So many times we let our failures define us and hinder us from moving forward. In this way, we can be our own worst enemy. But here are a few interesting facts to consider:

- Colonel Sanders faced over 1,000 rejections before his fried-chicken franchising efforts paid off. Wow! I'm not sure I would have made it past 100 rejections, let alone 1,000. I'm afraid if it had been me, my chicken recipe would have never made it past my kitchen.[4]
- Abraham Lincoln lost at least four elections before becoming president. Think of all the time and money he poured into each election only to lose, and we won't even talk about all the naysayers he must have encountered.[5]
- And then there is Thomas Edison who attempted 10,000 times to make a light bulb work. Talk about dogged determination. And think about how different our lives would be if he had quit after attempt 9,999. I'm thinking Yankee Candle stock might be significantly higher![6]

I remember the late Dr. Jerry Falwell, Chancellor of Liberty University and friend to all of us students, constantly telling us that failure is an event, not a person. It is not where you start in life but where you finish that matters. Failure is not falling down, but rather failure is staying down instead of picking yourself up, wiping off the dust, and with God's help continuing.

MOVE BEYOND YOUR PROBLEMS

The last obstacle and probably the most inhibiting foe to our dreams would be the problems we encounter. Just as the Everest climbers encountered paralyzing blows to their dreams, we also can experience hurt, rejection, and disappointment, all of which leave us reeling and even willing to forgo the journey toward our dreams.

Scripture is full of examples of people wrestling through the storms of life. One such story can be found in Mark 4:35-41 [HCSB]. Jesus and the disciples had just left the crowds and were now in a boat crossing over to the other side of the sea. All of a sudden, a fierce wind arose and the waves began crashing against the boat, threatening to sink it. The disciples became very afraid.

Now, you have to know these disciples were fishermen. They had endured many a storm on this sea, so it had to have been the storm of the century to rock their worlds. They looked frantically for Jesus and finally found Him asleep in the bottom of the boat. They woke Him and cried out, "Teacher, don't you care that we are going to die!" (Who says only women are dramatic?) Jesus got up, rebuked the wind, and simply said, "Peace, be still." Instantly, the winds ceased and the waters became still.

If Jesus can do that with a physical storm, how much more can He say, "Peace be still," and calm the storms in our lives? We all will face storms. Isaiah 43:2 [HCSB] says, "I will be with you when you pass through the waters, and when you pass through the rivers, they will not overwhelm you. You will not be scorched when you walk through the fire, and the flame will not burn you." Notice it does not say *if* you pass through the waters or the fire; it says I will be with you *when* you pass through the waters. As I have said before, problems are a part of life, and it's what we do with what we face that has the power to take us to the mountaintop or keep us in the valley.

PRESS INTO JESUS

Just recently, I was traveling to West Virginia to speak and sing at a women's event. I hesitantly got into my car, knowing that I was setting out for a weekend of ministry with nothing left to give. It had been an extremely exhausting and discouraging week for me—a week where I truly felt I was losing a piece of my heart each day as I helped the family that so lovingly raised me grapple with the heart-wrenching reality of Alzheimer's.

As I drove through the huge mountain passes, I found myself gripping the steering wheel for all I was worth and feeling as though I were hanging on for dear life. Worries overwhelmed me and fear threatened to take over—fear that something bad would happen while I was away and fear that I would not be able to minister to these ladies who had planned and prepared for this weekend with great anticipation.

When I arrived to do the concert that night, as tired, weary, and broken as I was, all I could do was just beg God to take over and minister to the women. And that is exactly what He did! Jesus showed up and took over, and many women received Him as their Savior and many found hope for the storms that were raging in their lives. I may not have had anything to give within myself, but God specializes in taking our weaknesses and turning them around to bring glory to His name.

I can't even begin to tell you how blessed I was that weekend. I went home so different from how I left. I went home recharged and filled up, ready to face the challenges ahead. My circumstances hadn't changed, but my hurting heart had been renewed by God's grace.

What are you facing in your life? A marriage that is falling apart? An illness that is ravaging your body? An addiction that you can't overcome? Abuse from your past? The loss of a loved one? I don't know what your heartache is, but I do know that God's grace is enough. It's enough for today's battles and beyond, enough to see you through whatever you are facing.

So many times our problems take center stage in our lives causing us to relinquish our dreams and threatening to steal our future. But it doesn't have to be that way! For in those difficult times, when we can hardly take another step, if we will press into Jesus and cry out to Him, He will show up and do the miraculous. Our desperate moments can truly become our greatest opportunities to rise above our circumstances with God's help and to bring the greatest glory to His name.

Dream Weaving

All of us face obstacles that must be overcome in the pursuit of our dreams. Whether it's our insecurities, fears, failures, or even problems that come along the way, we can each be derailed from our dreams if we do not learn how to stay the course regardless of our circumstances. Exercising vision beyond our circumstances, determination despite all odds, and reliance on the One who will see us through is what it takes to reach the summit of our dreams.

Have you ever sat down and really thought through your vision for your life? Take time this week to find a quiet place to contemplate and write down your vision for your future.

_____

_____

_____

_____

_____

_____

_____

_____

_____

_____

_____

_____

_____

_____

_____

Do you tend to see the negative or the positive in circumstances? Would you categorize yourself as being like the ten spies or like Caleb and Joshua? Take a few moments to think through situations that you may see pessimistically and ask God to help you see victory through His eyes.

_____

_____

_____

_____

_____

_____

_____

_____

_____

_____

_____

_____

_____

_____

Are you ever plagued by fear and insecurity? Take a moment to list what those fears and insecurities are and commit right now not to let another day be tainted by these dream-destroying foes.

_____

_____

_____

_____

_____

_____

_____

_____

_____

_____

_____

_____

_____

_____

_____

_____

Do you struggle with feelings of failure? Remind yourself that it is not a failure to fall; it's a failure to stay there. Write down Proverbs 24:16: "Though a righteous man falls seven times, he will get up." Place that in a visible spot to strengthen you each day. Remember, this is not a quick fix or where we surrender our problems to God once and for all. It is something we need to do each day, each hour, and maybe even each moment in the midst of our storms.

_____

_____

_____

_____

_____

_____

_____

_____

_____

_____

_____

_____

What are the struggles you are facing in your life? Write out a prayer to God acknowledging your pain and your dependence on Him. Thank Him for His grace that is enough for today, and then grab hold of that grace with all you have inside.

_____

_____

_____

_____

_____

_____

_____

_____

_____

_____

_____

_____

_____

_____

Have you ever been discouraged by someone shooting down your dreams? How are you when others share the dreams of their hearts? Do you cheer them on or give them every reason why it won't work? Determine right now not to let the opinions of others dictate your dreams. And for goodness sake, be a dream preserver and encourager to those around you. Think of two people this week whom you can take time to call, email, or visit in person, and speak a positive word to them. You might just be the one who spurs them on to greatness.

_____

_____

_____

_____

_____

_____

_____

_____

_____

_____

Chapter 5

This Will I Choose

EVERY DAY WE MAKE CHOICES.

We choose whether to get out of bed, what to wear, what we will eat, which activities we will participate in, and how we will respond to others, just to name a few. However, upon closer examination and just under the surface of all of our actions lie the murky waters of what we believe—what we believe about ourselves, about other people, and about the world we live in. These fundamental thoughts hold the power to either unlock the proper mindset needed to keep us moving toward our dreams or to stop us dead in our tracks.

Have you ever thought about how your thoughts impact your dreams? Have you ever considered the domino effect of how your dreams then affect your actions, which in turn determines your future and ultimately defines your destiny?

There is a direct correlation between how we view ourselves

and how we live out the dreams God has called us to. Proverbs 23:7 [KJV] says, "As a man thinketh in his heart, so is he." Essentially, you are what you think.

Let's face it: we live in a very negative world that focuses on what's wrong, what's ugly, what hurts, and what can't be done. But if you take time to observe successful people, you will see that most are positive and enthusiastic. I don't think you will find them obsessed with negativity and what they can't accomplish. Quite contrarily, successful people know who they are and are comfortable in their own skin. How much more should we as Christians have confidence in living out our dreams? After all, we have God abiding in us and working through us. What more could we ever need?

CHOOSE TO BELIEVE IN YOURSELF

Believing in ourselves is crucial to living out our dreams and our purpose. Now, I'm not talking about exalting ourselves or constantly singing our own praises. No, definitely not that. What I am talking about is an underlying confidence that we are uniquely made and have distinctive talents, ideas, and abilities that were given to us by God.

Often, people who are confident can seem prideful while those who are constantly putting themselves down and who are unable to accept a compliment are considered to be humble. I once heard a speaker make a bold point that I never forgot. He said that those who are constantly focusing on their insecurities, putting themselves down, and paralyzing themselves with fears of failure are actually the ones struggling with pride because the focus is always on themselves—what they can't do, what they don't have, and what they will never be—rather than on who God has created them to be and what He has called them to do.

Here's the key to relinquishing our insecurities and embracing a healthy confidence—knowing it's not about WHO we are and it's all about WHOSE we are.

Knowing who we are in Christ is powerful, for it can break the bonds of insecurity, fear, and even failure, which often hold us captive and keep us from attaining our dreams.

At the beginning of time, when God created man, He created us in His very image. May I be so bold to say that when we choose not to accept who He has created us to be and instead choose to focus on what we feel doesn't measure up, we are insulting our Creator? He uniquely made us and created us exactly the way we are for a distinct purpose that He planned even before the foundations of the earth. So, rather than spending our lives wrestling with our pride and insecurity, why not choose to be confident in how God made us, how He sees us, and how He wants to use us for His purposes?

CHOOSE TO BE CONFIDENT

If you look at Proverbs 31, you will see a woman who knew who she was and had the confidence to live it out. You don't have to read very far to be even a little envious of this industrious lady! Everything she had her hand in turned out to be successful! Her family revered her and called her blessed; her husband praised her, and she was known all throughout the city for her impeccable integrity and her undeniable accomplishments. What I find interesting is that not once do you read about her second guessing herself, questioning her giftedness, or giving up in defeat. No, it is quite the contrary. This woman never stopped using what God had given her to live out what He had called her to.

All throughout the chapter, this amazing woman selects wool, works with willing hands, brings her food from afar, rises while it is night, provides food for her household, evaluates and buys a field, plants a vineyard with her earnings, draws on her strength, reveals her arms are strong, knows that her merchandise is good, extends her hand to the spinning staff, reaches out to the poor and needy, is not afraid for her household, makes bed coverings and clothing in fine linens, sells garments in the city, delivers belts to the merchants, opens her mouth with wisdom and instructions, and watches over the activities of her household. How does one woman accomplish all of this? She accomplishes all of this because she doesn't waste time standing around wringing her hands on what she does or does not have; instead, she is confident in how God made her, how He gifted her, and how He will use her.

Could the Proverbs 31 woman have accomplished all that she did if she did not have her confidence in God? I highly doubt it. Thus, we can see from her example that, not only is it okay to be confident in who we are in Christ, it is essential to our success.

Imagine if we really embraced the fact that we are children of the King. I have a feeling we would think, believe, and live differently. Everything rides on finding our confidence in Him, so it is so important to nail it down in our hearts once and for all and apply it to our thoughts each day. When I was in graduate school, I was given a handout with an essay on it that so beautifully paints a picture of just how special we are to God:

In all the world there is nobody like you. Since the beginning of time, there has never been another person like you. Nobody has your smile. Nobody has your eyes, your hair, your hands, or your voice. You're special.

No one thinks just like you do. In all of time, there has been no one who laughs like you, no one who cries like you and what makes you laugh and cry will never provoke identical laughter and tears from anybody else, ever.

You are the only one in God's creation with your set of natural abilities. There will always be somebody who is better at one of the things you are good at, but no one in the universe can reach the quality of your combination of talents, ideas, natural abilities, and spiritual abilities.

Like a room full of instruments, some may excel alone, but none can match the symphony sound of the Body of Christ when all are played together because God set the members, every one of them in the Body, as it hath pleased Him. Through all of eternity, no one will ever walk, talk, look, think, or do exactly like you. You're special.

You're rare. And as in all rarity, there is great value. Because of your great rare value, you need not attempt to imitate others. You should accept, yes, celebrate your differences. You're special.

Continue to realize it's not an accident that you're special. Continue to see that God created you special for a very special purpose. He called you out and ordained you to a calling that is His special plan for your life. Out of all the billions of applicants, only one is qualified. Only one has the combination of what it takes.

Just as surely as every snowflake that falls has a perfect design and no two designs are the same, so it is within the Body of Christ also. No two believers are the same, and without each member the Body would be lacking and God's plan would be incomplete. Ask the Father to teach you His divine plan for your life and that it may

stand forth revealed to you as it should unfolding in perfect sequence and perfect order in such a way as to bring the greatest glory to His name. You're special.
—Author Unknown

You are special, and God has a special purpose that only you are qualified for and that only you can carry out. If you struggle with confidence, choose to make choices each day to change. Norman Vincent Peale once said, "If you will change your thoughts, you can change your world." The choice is up to you.

CHOOSE TO CHANGE

Maybe you are wondering, *How do I choose to change thoughts and feelings that I have had my entire life?* That's a fair question and one that necessitates an answer.

When I was in college finishing up my Master's Degree in counseling, I had to do an internship before I could graduate. After looking at numerous places, I decided on a residential program for pregnant teenage girls who need assistance in a facility called the Godparent Home in Lynchburg, Virginia.

Each week, I spent hours with these girls (some as young as thirteen years old), counseling them as they grappled with the life-changing decision of whether to parent or to place their babies for adoption. While this was the urgent issue at hand, it didn't take long for a host of other issues to surface—issues such as anorexia/bulimia, cutting, suicidal thoughts, and other forms of depression.

As I worked with these girls, I began to see a common thread among them. They didn't know who they were in Christ; they all struggled with self-worth; and not one of them could break free from the self-defeating thoughts and behaviors that had taken over their young lives. My heart broke for these girls, and I began to pray earnestly for each of them daily. I also asked God to show me how I could help them. His answer was very simple, yet effective as He placed in my heart a process I call the 3 Rs, which consists of Recognizing, Replacing, and Repeating the truth. This became a tool I used with these girls to help them assess and change their unhealthy thought patterns.

CHOOSE TO RECOGNIZE UNHEALTHY THOUGHTS

Finally brothers, whatever is true, whatever is honorable, whatever is just, whatever is pure, whatever is lovely, whatever is commendable—if there is any moral excellence and if there is any praise—dwell on these things.

—Philippians 4:8 HCSB

First, we learned how to RECOGNIZE unhealthy thoughts with

Scripture being our standard.

What a perfect standard to test our thoughts against. I would tell the girls, "If your thoughts do not measure up to these standards, then you need to dismiss them immediately. Just because you think something doesn't mean it's true or that it has to stay in your mind. You have a choice of what you choose to dwell on and what you choose to discard."

CHOOSE TO REPLACE THE LIES WE BELIEVE

Once we found that a thought was not healthy, we would then REPLACE the unhealthy thought with the truth. Since God's Word is the source of all truth, that is where we must go to replace the unhealthy thoughts that have wallpapered our minds. The Bible is full of verses to combat our unhealthy ways of thinking, and there are many resources out there to help us find these verses. One of my favorites is Bible Gateway, an online Bible resource.

So here's an example of how we implement replacing our unhealthy thoughts with the truth: if one of the girls were struggling with fear, we would look up every verse that pertained to fear, pick a few favorites, and then write them down on index cards, making them easily available to pull out in the midst of a fearful moment. For instance, 2 Timothy 1:7 [KJV] says, "For God has not given us a spirit of fear, but of power and of love and of a sound mind." From this verse, we can see that fear is not from God, and if it's not from Him, then it must be from the enemy. When we break it down like this, rejecting unhealthy thoughts and replacing them with God's truth becomes much simpler.

CHOOSE TO REPEAT THE TRUTH

The last R is what truly solidifies change. We must REPEAT the truth continuously. None of us became the way we are overnight, so it is going to take time and practice before we can experience real change. Consistently recognizing what is not healthy, replacing it with the truth of God's Word, and then repeating it over and over until it becomes a way of life will put us well on the road to healthier thoughts and beliefs.

CHOOSE TO TRANSFORM YOUR SELF-TALK

Not only do our thoughts impact our actions, but our internal dialogue—often referred to as our self-talk—plays a huge role in setting us up for success or failure. When we tell ourselves that we can't do something, at that moment, we are probably right because we have already made the decision that we can't. Instead of telling ourselves we can't, we can replace that internal dialogue with Philippians 4:13 [NKJV], which says, "I can do ALL things through Christ who strengthens me" (emphasis added). Can you see how changing what we say to ourselves truly can empower us and open the door to a whole world of possibilities?

I recently came across a wonderful resource online that

You Say. God Says. Bible Verse

I can't figure it out.	I will direct your steps.	Proverbs 3:5-6
I am too tired.	I will give you rest.	Matthew 11:28-30
It's impossible.	All things are possible.	Luke 18:27
Nobody loves me.	I love you.	John 3:16
I can't forgive myself.	I forgive you.	Romans 8:1
It's not worth it.	It will be worth it.	Romans 8:28
I'm not smart enough.	I will give you wisdom.	I Corinthians 1:30
I'm not able.	I am able.	II Corinthians 9:8
I can't go on.	My grace is sufficient.	II Corinthians 12:9
I can't do it.	You can do all things.	Philippians 4:13
I can't manage.	I will supply your needs.	Philippians 4:19
I am afraid.	I have not given you fear.	II Timothy 1:7
I feel all alone.	I will never leave you.	Hebrews 13:5

Figure 1: Chart modified from [iBelieve.com, Inspirations, "You say, God says" chart] http://www.ibelieve.com/inspirations/you-say-god-says.html (accessed December 1, 2014).

addresses some of the common self-defeating thoughts we often tell ourselves and refutes each of these points with God's Truths. (See chart on page 85.) There is power in what we think and what we say. Both our thoughts and words can either build us up and empower us as we move toward our dreams or they can tear us down in defeat. That is why we must not allow ourselves to focus on the negative but embrace positive and uplifting thoughts and words that speak life into our hopes and dreams.

CHOOSE TO GUARD YOUR MIND

When was the last time you took an inventory of your thoughts and beliefs? This is so important for all of us to do, for even when we are firmly grounded we can let our guard down and before long have our thoughts go awry.

1 Peter 5:8 [KJV] says, "Be sober, be vigilant; because your adversary the devil walks about like a roaring lion, seeking whom he may devour." Notice that last word *devour*. This is a pretty strong word that paints a very vivid picture in my mind. Maybe I have watched too many Animal Planet documentaries with my animal-obsessed daughter on the prowess of lions as they attack (ugh!), but when I think of the word *devour* I most definitely picture a ruthless lion savagely ripping apart its prey.

Although our enemy doesn't hunt us down physically as a lion would, I believe he is ruthless and ferocious in how he attacks our minds. Just as he planted the seeds of doubt and uncertainty in Eve's mind in the Garden of Eden, he still works overtime doing the same to us today. It is his mission to infiltrate our thoughts and cause us to question, doubt, and give up on our dreams. In doing so, we are stuck on the sidelines and kept from all that God has for us.

Now, don't think for a second I am ending this chapter with us fearing lion attacks and flaming darts of Satan. Here's what we must never lose sight of no matter what the enemy tries to bring our way: We already have the victory in Jesus Christ our Lord! As 1 John 4:4 [KJV] says, "Greater is He that is in you than he that is in the world."

So, the next time your thoughts threaten to submerge you and keep your dreams at bay, hold your head high and choose to believe who you are in Christ. Here's what you can hang on to: You are created in God's image, you are His child, and He loves you fiercely and has a phenomenal plan for your life.

Let this be your mindset and let this be your mantra—God is for you! He is for you when you feel unworthy! He is for you when you struggle to believe! He is for you when you doubt your future! He is for you when you want to give up on your dream! So, let go of negativity and the thoughts that hold you back, and boldly chase the dreams that God has placed in your heart! The future ahead is bright for those who know who they are and who make the choice to be positive and believe!

Dream Weaving

Whether we realize it or not, our thoughts in many ways define who we are and often determine our destiny. Simply stated, what we choose to believe about ourselves sets us up for either success or failure in life. We can choose to embrace negative thoughts that tear us down or we can choose to find our confidence in the One who created us in His image, loves us fiercely, and has an incredible plan for our lives. The choice is up to us.

How do you see yourself? What are your talents and abilities? And it's okay to list them—you are not being prideful or self-promoting. You are simply acknowledging the gifts God has given you.

Do you struggle with feelings of insecurity or inadequacy? Take a stab at doing the 3 Rs. List the unhealthy, self-defeating thoughts you rehearse in your mind and then look up verses to combat them and to replace them with the truth.

_____

_____

_____

_____

_____

_____

_____

_____

_____

_____

_____

_____

_____

_____

Write out a prayer to the Lord asking Him to re-wallpaper the walls of your mind with His truths rather than the lies of Satan.

_____

_____

_____

_____

_____

_____

_____

_____

_____

_____

_____

_____

_____

_____

_____

Chapter 6

Dancing in the Rain

MY COLLEGE SINGING GROUP HAD BEEN TRAVELING on the road for weeks, all nine of us packed into a passenger van like sardines. Every night we had a different church to sing at, in a different city, and often a different state. After traveling all day, we would sing our hearts out, and then we would pack up our equipment and each head to a home with complete strangers from the church who signed up to host us. As crazy as this may sound, I really enjoyed the adventure and the unpredictability of it all.

For some reason, any unusual host-family experiences almost always happened to me. One such host home experience that will always line the hallways of my mind took place after a concert one evening in Pennsylvania. Upon arrival at my host family's house, they brought my luggage in and set it on the floor in the living room. *Hmm. That must mean the bedroom is small and doesn't have any extra space for my suitcase*, I thought. The family then took me through the living room, the dining room, the kitchen, and then out the back door where they proceeded to show me a Mack truck that would be my bed for the night.

At first, I thought they were kidding and began to laugh. However, I quickly realized they weren't laughing. They were serious. *Wow!* I had never slept in the cab of a Mack truck before.

It was very tight quarters, to say the least, and not the comfiest set up, but it definitely made for a great story the next day when I joined up with the team. My teammates could not believe I had slept in a Mack truck.

Now, before I go any further, for posterity sake I must include my husband's favorite part of the story, much to my embarrassment. Since it was so late when we arrived at the house, my host family assumed that I had already had dinner, so they said goodnight to me and went to bed. As I got all situated in the truck (not that there was much to situate) my hunger pangs became undeniable. I tried to ignore them but couldn't. Finally, I made the crazy decision to sneak back into the house to try to find a snack.

As quiet as a mouse, I began to rummage around in the kitchen for anything that would suffice. Moments later, I heard someone else making their way to the kitchen. In that instant I had a choice to either be honest and explain what I was doing and humbly ask for a snack or to panic and do something very different. Unfortunately, I chose the latter and quickly jumped into the pantry and shut the door. I immediately knew I had made the wrong decision, sort of like picking the "Price Is Right" door that gives you a bottle of Pepto Bismol instead of the trip to Hawaii. But this was much worse, for I knew that in one crazy instance I had put everything on the line. *What would I do if someone opened the pantry door that my nose was now pressed against? Would I hand them a bag of chips and fumble through a mumbled excuse for hiding in their pantry?*

The next few moments felt like hours. I think I surrendered to those jungles of Africa several times. I would do anything if that pantry door would just not open. I listened to someone open the refrigerator and then patiently waited while they ate a snack. Finally, what seemed like an eternity later, they made their way back to bed. Suddenly, I was no longer hungry. In fact, that Mack truck never looked so good!

Then, there was another unforgettable time when our team showed up at a church in Atlanta. This church was located in a very affluent part of town. Just from the appearance of the church, I knew we had hit the jackpot of host families.

As families began to arrive in Mercedes, BMWs, Cadillacs, and such, I would be lying if I did not say my hopes were very high for an incredible host-home experience. I had visions of having my own comfy bed and private bathroom, perhaps even a dip in a swimming pool or a soak in a relaxing jacuzzi tub. I imagined all of this, that is, until I spotted one beat-up van with about ten children running around it.

As soon as my eyes landed on all the commotion, I instantly knew what my fate would be. Sure enough, as our names were called out with the families we were each assigned to it was determined that the family with ten kids was all mine. I slept that night in a bunk bed with two kids above me and one right beside me all snuggled up together on plastic sheets.

What do you envision when you think of plastic sheets? Let me tell you what I think just by saying I slept on the edge of the bunk bed all night. When I arrived at the church the next morning before our concert, it was amazing to hear of all the master suites, jacuzzi tubs, and guest cottages that my teammates all enjoyed. God truly has a sense of humor!

I promise I have a reason for sharing these crazy stories besides just providing some humor. In both situations, I had a choice to make. I could perceive the situation as the worst thing ever, allow myself to have a bad attitude about it, and just be miserable, or I could choose to find the humor in it and know that it wouldn't last forever.

We all face situations in life that fall short of our expectations and can derail us from our dreams. What we choose to believe and perceive about our circumstances significantly contributes to our success or our failure. The choice is up to us.

What we choose to believe and perceive about our circumstances significantly contributes to our success or our failure.

EXPECTATIONS CAN DECEIVE US

John 11 tells a sobering story of two sisters who were hurting, disappointed, and maybe even disillusioned as their expectations were radically denied. Mary and Martha had watched helplessly as their brother Lazarus became gravely ill. Desperate for a miracle, they immediately sent word to Jesus of Lazarus' plight. They had seen Jesus perform many miracles and just knew in their hearts that He would intervene for them.

However, this script didn't play out at all the way the sisters had hoped. Jesus got the word about Lazarus and stayed where He was for two extra days. It was during those two days that Lazarus took his last breath and died.

I'm sure in the ensuing days Mary and Martha struggled with the bitter ache of being denied the one thing they had asked of Jesus. He loved Lazarus. *Why didn't He come right away to rescue him when He had done it for so many others that weren't even close to Him?* Perhaps these and many more questions swirled around in their minds.

By the time Jesus arrived on the scene, Lazarus had already been in the tomb for four days. Both Martha and Mary couldn't conceal their grief or their disappointment as they choked out what their hearts cried, "Lord, if you had been here, [our] brother wouldn't have died" (John 11:21 HCSB). Jesus answered them by saying, "I am the resurrection and the life. The one who believes in Me, even if he dies, will live" (John 11:25 HCSB). Thinking Jesus was referring to the second resurrection, the sisters had more than likely given up on the hope of seeing their brother alive again anytime soon. Jesus saw their sorrow and wept with them, which I'm sure put to rest any chance of a miracle in their minds.

What the grieving sisters didn't realize was that the stage was being set for Jesus to do the unexpected and to perform the miraculous.

The story concludes with Jesus entering Lazarus' tomb and shouting, "Lazarus, come forth!" Instantly, Lazarus came forth still bound with linen strips and wrapped in burial cloths. There is no doubt the stunned crowd did a double take just to be sure they weren't dreaming all of this. No, it was not a dream. Jesus showed up and far exceeded anyone's hopes and dreams.

A powerful take away of this story is this: just because things don't go our way, as we think they should, it doesn't mean that God has forgotten us or that His plan is not perfect. Mary and Martha envisioned Jesus dropping everything, rushing to their rescue, and healing Lazarus from his sickness. But God had a greater plan for His greater glory. Jesus came after the fact so He could raise Lazarus from the dead, thus resulting in a much greater miracle and more glory to His name!

So many times I can be like Mary and Martha—seeing my circumstances through the lens of my limited perspective, often resulting in disappointment and discouragement. It really all comes down to trust. Do I trust Jesus and His plan? Am I willing to let go of my script of how I think everything should go and allow Him to freely write on the pages of my life? When we relinquish our expectations and control, Jesus is free to show up and far exceed our hopes and dreams.

When we relinquish our expectations and control, Jesus is free to show up and far exceed our hopes and dreams.

PERSPECTIVE CAN FREE US

Just recently, my family and I had one last hurrah before school started by taking a short getaway to the beach. Our daughter, Emma, had informed us that in all of her seven years of living she had only been to the beach one time for a few hours. I know what you're thinking—major parent fail!

You've probably surmised that I am not a die-hard beach girl (which is probably accurate). While I love the idea of the beach—the crashing waves, the breeze, the warm sun, the laid-back, fun atmosphere, etc.—the reality of the massive amounts of sand found for days to follow forces me to grin and bear it as the sand covers our bodies, our towels, our bags, and even our car. On the other hand, my husband, Robb, loves it all. Still, he can get his entire beach experience filled in just two short hours, and then he is ready to move on. However, as any dutiful parents would, we laid all of our reservations aside and embarked on this two-day beach adventure filled with big plans for all kinds of fun for our daughter.

As we drove through torrential rain to get there, I studied the impending forecast only to find two straight days of rain and thunderstorms ahead of us. My mind began to race with "plan B" options. But when the beach is what your seven-year-old has been dreaming of and thinking about for weeks, there is no plan B. Rain or shine, stormy or serene, there was no turning back. The beach would be our destiny for the next two days.

Since we were practically driving through a monsoon to get there, we decided to take our time and grab some lunch and also stop for some beach essentials. You know, the boogie board, the token pail and shovel that you pay ten dollars for (all the while kicking yourself for not grabbing the stack of them at home), bottled waters, and all the infamous beach snacks that you can't live without—all essential parts of the perfect beach excursion, I might add.

We finally arrived at the much-anticipated resort during the late afternoon, which gave us time to get settled and scout out the beach that we would be calling home for the next two days. After dinner and ice cream, we nestled in our beds with visions of surfboards and sand castles all dancing in our heads.

Hours later, we awoke to an 80 percent chance of rain forecast and mostly cloudy skies at best. "That's okay," we cheered. We were at the beach, and we were going to make the most of it. We packed our beach bag, donned our bathing suits, slathered ourselves up with sunscreen, and we were on our way with an optimistic skip in our step.

Upon arrival, we happily set up camp, rented chairs and an umbrella, and officially made our beach debut. Robb and Emma jumped the waves as I cheered them on. We searched for crabs and starfish, made sand castles, and, in the midst of all of our beach fun, failed to notice the dark clouds rolling in until they were right upon us.

As the threatening clouds grew darker and the rain began to descend, I couldn't help but notice three very distinct reactions from our fellow beachgoers. First, there were those who panicked and quickly scurried to gather all of their carefully laid out beach accessories and ran as fast as they could indoors, away from the storm—their high hopes and dreams of a perfect beach day shattered by the fierceness of the wind and rain.

Then, there were those like me who hunkered down under the umbrella all the while hoping and praying the storm would quickly pass by, yet disappointed by the interruption it caused to their plans.

Lastly, there was Robb and Emma. They chose not to let the storm affect their dreams for the day. They ran, chased the waves, and danced in the rain, making the most of every moment despite the less than ideal circumstances.

As I listened to my family's laughter and watched them chase each other into the ocean, I couldn't help but wonder if this whole beach experience was a picture of how it is in our lives when the unexpected storms come along. We all have such high hopes and dreams for how we want things to be. We make meticulous plans for our dreams, yet sometimes storms come along and threaten to hijack everything.

It is in those disappointing moments that we can choose how we will perceive and react to the storm. We can panic and immediately give up on our most cherished dreams—seeing the storm as a permanent and invincible foe in our lives. We can hunker down and wait for the storm to pass, fixating on the disruption to our plans. Or we can see the storm as a passing inconvenience but not a dream destroyer. We can choose to keep living, to keep dancing, and to make the most of every minute of this adventure called life.

The choice is really up to us. It's all about perspective, and it's all about trust. So, if you will excuse me while I leave my umbrella, I've got some dancing in the rain to catch up on.

Dream Weaving

At some point in our lives, we all face situations that can disappoint us, fall short of our expectations, and even tempt us to give up on our most cherished dreams. How we choose to perceive our circumstances ultimately determines whether we rise above our disappointments or give in to defeat. It all comes down to trust. When we can't see the big picture, are we going to trust the One who can? When things don't go the way we planned, are we willing to let go of our expectations and trust God's sovereign hand? Choosing to trust and to give up our control allows Jesus to show up and freely write upon the pages of our lives a story that goes far beyond our hopes and dreams.

How do you often perceive people and situations? Do you see the good or do you automatically assume the worst?

_____

_____

_____

_____

_____

_____

_____

_____

_____

_____

_____

_____

_____

_____

_____

_____

Do you struggle with trusting God's plan when it doesn't make sense or adhere to your hopes and dreams? Think back to a time when what you thought was God not coming through for you actually was Him at work doing something greater than you could have ever dreamed. Take a moment and thank Him for working all things for our good.

_____

_____

_____

_____

_____

_____

_____

_____

_____

_____

_____

_____

_____

_____

How do you react when your expectations are not met? Do you panic? Hunker down and wait on your dreams? Or do you fully engage yourself into living out your dreams regardless of the circumstances?

_____

_____

_____

_____

_____

_____

_____

_____

_____

_____

_____

_____

_____

_____

Write out a prayer to God reaffirming your full trust in His sovereign master plan for your life. Look for everyday situations this week where you can exchange dashed expectations with trust in God, believing in what He is doing rather than focusing on the disappointment you feel in that situation.

_____

_____

_____

_____

_____

_____

_____

_____

_____

_____

_____

_____

Choose to dance in the rain. Whatever has interrupted your dream or plan is no surprise to God. Perhaps He wants to use it to reveal Himself to you in a greater way. Write out Romans 8:28 in the space below. Write it on an index card as well and put it where you will see it each day. Let it be a reminder that God has all things under His control. When you face moments you can't control and that do not adhere to your plan, take comfort in knowing He is always in control.

_____

_____

_____

_____

_____

_____

_____

_____

_____

_____

_____

Chapter 7

Faith to Believe

*Faith is seeing above the invisible,
believing the unbelievable, and receiving
the impossible.*
—*Corrie Ten Boom*

HAVE YOU EVER WONDERED WHAT THE FUTURE looks like, where you will be in five, ten, or twenty years? If only we had a sneak peek of the motion picture of our lives. How much better would we be at making decisions if we knew where they all led?

Unfortunately, there are no such films, no "Back to the Future" episodes, and no crystal balls. What we do have access to, however, is a God who is the director of our futures. If we place an unabashed faith in Him, we will find that He always does as He promises, and in Ephesians 3:20, He promises to do exceedingly and abundantly more than we could ever ask or think.

God wants to push us past the boundaries of ordinary into the realm of extraordinary living. Extraordinary as defined by Webster is "going beyond what is usual, regular, or customary."[8] I believe it is living beyond the mundane, above mediocrity, and in the center of all that He has called us to. This can only be accomplished in a life that is built on a foundation of faith.

What is faith? Faith is complete dependence on God. People with faith have a different outlook on life. They see more than just the circumstances they are facing; they see God working through them. Oswald Chambers defines faith as "the inborn capacity to see God behind everything."[9] Imagine if we saw God behind everything. Suddenly mountains could be reduced to foothills, storms could be calmed, peace could drown out chaos, and hope could replace desperation.

People with faith see more than the circumstances they are facing; they see God working.

I remember learning an acronym for faith when I was a child in Sunday school—Full Assurance In The Heart. While it was a great way to describe faith, it falls just a little short in defining it. Full assurance in the heart about what? I believe it is full assurance in the heart that God is sovereign and in control of our lives and truly has our best interests at the center of His plan for us. Does that mean we will never face a problem and everything will always be rosy? Hardly so! What it does mean is that we will never face our struggles alone and that God is our source for everything and will help us navigate the stormy seas.

It's important to note that faith does not begin with us; it begins with God. Mark 9:17-24 [HCSB] tells a story of a desperate father who brought his son to Jesus. This son had been possessed by a spirit since childhood that made him unable to speak and caused him to convulse and foam at the mouth. Many times he was cast by the spirit into fire or water as it tried to destroy him. The father had tried everything to no avail. His last hope was Jesus.

As the father begged Jesus to have compassion on them and to help his son, Jesus responded by saying, "Everything is possible to the one who believes." Immediately, the father of the boy cried out, "I do believe! Help my unbelief." In that instant, Jesus heard the desperate father's cry and rebuked the spirit. The spirit came out of the boy shrieking. It made him convulse violently and then dropped him like a rag doll. Many thought the boy was dead, but Jesus took him by the hand and raised him up.

This story holds an encouraging message for us, and it's that God cares for every detail of our lives. God will intervene when there is no other way. Nothing is impossible to those who believe. But perhaps the greatest salve for my weary soul is found in "I believe. Help my unbelief."

There are times in all of our lives when our faith wavers, when the waves crash over us and we can barely stay afloat, let alone courageously live out our dreams. I think God knew we would need to know that we can ask Him for the faith to believe. Perhaps that is why He even included this story in the Bible to let us know that when we can't even muster the strength to find the faith that we need, God will come through and give us the faith to believe. Rather than beating ourselves up in those fragile moments of our faith, we need to get on our knees and ask our God for the faith to see us through.

Faith does not begin with us; it begins with God.

TAKE A LEAP OF FAITH

I can tell you of so many times in my life where God gave me the faith to believe when I couldn't find it within myself. One particular time that comes to mind is when God opened up the doors for me to record my first album in Nashville using some of the best musicians in the business. While I was so honored and humbled to have that level of talent involved in my album, I also knew this bigger opportunity would involve a bigger price tag.

We had a $40,000 recording budget with only $1,000 to put toward it at the time. I must tell you, this is not how I liked to operate. I liked having everything planned with the money in the bank before beginning. However, God had other plans.

I was working through the Bible study *Experiencing God* at

that time, and it kept challenging me to step out and do something for God that I did not have the resources or abilities to do so that He would be the only One who would receive the glory once it was accomplished. Yikes! This was definitely pushing me out of my comfort zone. I couldn't help but focus on the money and worry about how we would ever come up with it. Robb and I were newlyweds and traveling on the road without any surplus income. *What were we thinking even considering this?*

Despite my misgivings, God would not leave me alone on this and kept pushing us forward. Finally, I literally got on my knees and prayed, "Lord, I don't know how you are going to do this, but I believe! Please help my unbelief." I continued praying each day for God to give me the faith that I needed to trust Him. I also began a study on faith. What I soon realized was that the miracles Jesus performed were often a direct result of a person's faith.

For instance:

- Matthew 8:13: The man's servant was healed because he believed.
- Matthew 9:22: The woman who touched the hem of Jesus' garment was told that her faith healed her.
- Matthew 9:29: Jesus told the blind man whose sight was restored that according to his faith it would be done.

BELIEVE IN THE MIRACULOUS

As I read on, I found in Matthew 13:58 that Jesus did not do many miracles in His hometown because of their lack of faith. Then it hit me: I wonder how many miracles we miss out on because of our lack of faith. I wonder how many times has God been ready and willing to do the impossible in my life but I couldn't hold up my end of the deal and just believe.

The Bible says in Matthew 17:20 that if we have the faith of a mustard seed, nothing will be impossible for us. This is so much more than something God would *like* for us to do, for He tells us in Hebrews 11:6 that without faith it is *impossible* to please Him. Therefore, if we choose to worry and do not practice faith, we are not pleasing God. How convicting is that?

We are to live by faith and not by sight. A $40,000 album was impossible for Robb and me, but it was not impossible for God. All of a sudden, this was no longer about money; it was about faith. I began to pray less about our finances and more about the faith to believe that God was going to provide.

It didn't happen overnight, but slowly I felt the anxiety turn to excitement for how God would provide this miracle in just three short months. I tell you today that every single time we had a payment due the Lord brought the money in. We didn't have to beg, borrow, or steal. God sent it sometimes in the most unexpected ways. On one such time, we pulled up to a very small church, wondering how we would even pay our expenses for the trip and left after the concert with not only money for our expenses, but we had thousands to go toward the new album as well. Another example is when I walked to the mailbox one day to find an unexpected check sent to us for $1500. On and on it went, God blowing us away with His provision.

Three months from when we started, the entire project was paid for. Crazy, huh? Here's what I know: just as an earthly parent loves their children and wants to do nice things, our Father in Heaven wants even more to give us good gifts. (See Matthew 7:11.)

What good gifts do you need to ask or believe God for today? You have not because you ask not. Go ahead. Ask for the faith and then believe. He will show up and do the miraculous. And not only will your faith grow in the process, but the dreams of your heart will be reaffirmed and blaze even brighter as well!

TAP INTO A LIFE OF TRUST

Faith is not just an outlook; it's a way of life. In order to fully live out God's dreams, we have to understand there are several types of faith that must be deeply woven into the fabric of our lives. If we were to look at the faith of a child, we would see that it is often without doubt, without fear, and that it has complete confidence in the object of the child's trust. As we discussed in Chapter 1, we all had that kind of childlike faith in our dreams until we grew up. Somehow, in the process we lost sight of believing in a God of the impossible and chose to see our circumstances as improbable.

A trip down memory lane is always a good remedy for regaining our focus, for in doing so we will see that we can trust God because He has always been trustworthy. Not once has He left us, failed us, or rejected us, and He certainly isn't going to start now. The question is whether or not we trust Him.

The *365 Devotional Commentary* by Lawrence Richards takes Psalm 37 and explores what trust is and lists it as the following:

- Looking to God and doing good (vs. 3),
- Delighting in the Lord (vs. 4),
- Committing our ways to the Lord (vs. 5),
- Refraining from anger and wrath (vs. 8),
- Being satisfied with little (vs. 16),
- Giving generously to others (vs. 21),
- Turning from evil to do good (vs. 27),
- Planting God's Law in our hearts (vs. 31),
- Waiting for the Lord (vs. 34),
- Keeping His ways (vs. 34), and
- Taking refuge in the Lord (vs. 40).[10]

Some benefits of trusting God include:

- Receiving the desire of our hearts (vs. 4),
- Being vindicated (vs. 5-6),
- Inheriting the land (vs. 9),
- Finding peace (vs. 9),
- Being upheld by God (vs. 17),
- Enjoying plenty in the days of famine (vs. 19),
- Living securely (vs. 27),
- Never being forsaken by God (vs. 28),
- Not slipping (vs. 31),
- Having a future (vs. 37), and
- Being helped and delivered by God (vs. 40).[11]

How can we lose by placing our complete faith in a loving God who wants to take care of us and bless us? Just as you want your child to trust you implicitly, your Heavenly Father longs for you to do the same by placing your childlike faith in Him.

EMBRACE A LIVING FAITH

In order to experience all that God has for us, we also must have a living faith. In Amos 5:21-25, God reveals to the Israelites that He hated their sacrifices, despised their feast days, and refused to accept their offerings. The first time I read this passage, I thought, *Why in the world would God hate the very thing He commanded them to do?* Upon reading further, I quickly discovered it was because they were going through the motions with God. They were serving God out of a habit with a heart that was far from Him. They had a faith that was dead and dormant rather than a relationship that was alive and growing.

I wonder how many times we have been guilty of the same— doing things for God out of habit rather than from a heart of love. The truth is, we all know the right way to look, the right way to talk, and the right way to live. We can even reduce our faith to a list of rules and things we should and should not do, but God doesn't care about that. He doesn't want a faith from us that is steeped in tradition; He wants our hearts. He doesn't want our religion; He longs for a relationship with you and me that is real and personal. It is this relationship with Him that goes hand in hand with our faith. If we want to have faith that is unwavering and alive, our relationship with God must be the same. We can't have one without the other.

How is your faith today? But even more important, how is your relationship with God? Do you know Him in a real and personal way? You are only as close to Him as you choose to be. God is always willing and available.

Perhaps a story that illustrates this best is of a married couple driving along in their pickup truck. They had driven these roads for many a year, in the same truck, in the same town, in the same way. Early on in their marriage, hardly a day would pass when the wife wouldn't jump into the truck and scoot over as close as she possibly could and snuggle up to her man as they drove down the road. As the years passed, they still drove that same truck on the same roads in the same town. But then one day, she realized that she didn't sit close to him anymore. This really bothered her, so she looked at her husband and sweetly asked him why they no longer sat so close together in his truck. Holding the steering wheel, and with a twinkle in his eye, he said something simple, yet profound: "I never moved."

The fact of the matter is that God never moves away from us; we are the ones who can be like the Israelites and stray away from Him and ultimately miss out on God's best and the dreams and plans He has for our lives. But here's the good news: You are only one decision away from having a relationship with Him that is real and alive.

STEP INTO THE UNKNOWN

Probably one of the hardest aspects of pursuing our dreams is stepping into the unknown, for the unknown can often feel more like a risky and frivolous venture than a road to success. However, if you look at successful people, you will see they courageously went after their dreams without a guarantee of success. Think about Christopher Columbus making that voyage across the ocean. I'm sure people thought he was crazy and wasting his time, but oh, how wrong they were. What about the Wright brothers? What if they had never stepped out into the unknown? Think about how different our lives would be without air travel.

The Bible also gives many examples of people who stepped out in faith and had no idea where God was leading them or how it would even turn out. Imagine how Noah felt building an enormous ark before seeing a drop of rain. Then there's Daniel who refused the king's delicacies and would not back down from worshiping God, and as a result was thrown into the lion's den with no way out. I'm sure he was wondering what in the world God was up to. How about Shadrach, Meshach, and Abednego? They were thrown into the fiery furnace for choosing to worship God rather than bowing to King Nebuchadnezzar's golden image. I'm sure their faith was put to the test as the flames danced all around them. None of these people knew if they would even make it out alive, but they obeyed God and placed all of their faith in Him.

Now, we may not be facing floods, lions, or fiery furnaces, but there are times in all our lives when we can struggle with God's plans. I've shared that I like everything neatly laid out for me, but sometimes God wants us to step out in obedient faith— outside of our plans and into full reliance on Him—and to attempt God-sized tasks so that He is the only One to receive the glory. For it is when we step out into the unknown, trusting Him and believing Him for our very survival, that He can unleash His power and bring the greatest glory to His name.

In 1577, Sir Francis Drake was the first person to circumnavigate the world. This was his prayer as he set sail:

> *Disturb us, O Lord, when we are too well pleased with ourselves, when our dreams have come true because we dreamed too little, when we arrived safely because we sailed too close to the shore.*
>
> *Disturb us, O Lord, to dare more boldly, to venture on wider seas where storms will show Your mastery; where losing sight of land, we shall find the stars.*
>
> *We ask You to push back the horizons of our hopes and push us in the future in strength, courage, hope, and love. This we ask in the name of our Captain, who is Jesus Christ.*[12]

What a great prayer for our lives today! As hard as it can be setting sail into the oceans of the unknown, I certainly don't want my dreams to go unfulfilled because I have stayed too close to shore. I don't want to miss out on the best dreams that God has for me because I chose to play it safe and only go after dreams I knew were possible.

Hence, the question we must all answer: what would you step out and do if you weren't obsessed with knowing how it would all turn out? What is God asking you to obediently step out in faith and do for His glory?

Jud Wilhite states that the most extraordinary and faith-filled people "are not the most talented but the most available. They are not the most powerful but the most servant-oriented. They are not the most driven but the most surrendered. They choose God's will in spite of their own. They choose God's power when they are weak and worn. They take the road less traveled and experience faith's transforming power."[13] This can all take place when we choose to exercise faith and step into the unknown, trusting God completely for the outcome.

SURRENDER YOUR BROKEN DREAMS

Right after 9/11, I was scheduled to speak and sing at a large Amway Conference. At the very end of my segment, they had a lady come up and share her story. Her name was Cheryl McGuiness. Cheryl shared that her husband was the pilot of the first airplane that hit the World Trade Center in New York City. She shared how devastating it was to hear the news of her husband's death and how heartbreaking it was to tell her children on that tragic day.

Cheryl and Tom had been high school sweethearts. They started a family after they married, and Tom was a wonderful husband and father. He had a great career as a pilot, and he was very active in their church and even taught a Bible study. Life was great—and then 9/11. Cheryl went on to share how difficult it was living life without Tom, but she shared something else that day that I never forgot. She said, "Every day when I wake up without Tom beside me, God is my very breath. He gives me exactly what I need for every moment without Tom."[14]

As she shared, you could have heard a pin drop. No one dared to move or breathe and interrupt the holiness of that moment— the holiness of God reaching down and receiving this woman's desperate faith and filling the innermost crevices of her broken heart with Him.

It is when we are broken and desperate that God can completely fill us and use us more than we ever could have imagined. As Cheryl finished speaking, people began to flood the front of the room as they got before God and asked for His touch in their lives. They too offered up their desperate faith and received His abundant grace. As I saw the tears and heard the whispers of their heartfelt prayers, it became so evident to me that we all have different backgrounds and different stories, but we all have one thing in common—we all need God. Without Him we are lost, but with Him we have everything.

There will always be desperate times in our lives and in our world. You can't help but see a world in need just by turning on the television at night with scenes of terrorists, bloodshed, natural disasters, and death. But no matter the circumstances, our source of hope and strength will never change. In John 16:33 [HCSB], Jesus says, "In Me you may have peace. You will have suffering in this world. Be courageous! I have conquered the world."

You may only be able to offer desperate faith today, but in God's economy there is no greater place to be. As was discussed in the very first chapter, God can take our broken hearts and turn them into a shining example of hope, healing, and purpose. The depths of our pain can become the passion of our hearts when we surrender our broken dreams to the One who holds our every moment in the palm of His sovereign hand.

A LIFE TRANSFORMED

There is one last type of faith that we must experience before we can truly know the extraordinary plans God has for us, and that is saving faith—faith to believe and receive Christ as our personal Savior. For some, this decision comes immediately upon hearing about the gift of salvation that Jesus offers, while others can grapple with this decision for a lifetime. So simple for some, yet so complicated for others. This was made so real to me years ago through a man named Mr. Smith.

We had just bought a leftover lot in an established neighborhood in town. We were so thrilled not only to build, but also to own our very first home. We could hardly wait to move in! The day finally came to move in, and every day thereafter felt like Christmas. We loved our little corner of the world. We were so excited to meet our neighbors and quickly found that all of them had lived there for many years. As we met each family, we learned a lot of the history and background of each of them.

Right away, we found our next-door neighbor Mr. Smith especially intriguing. He was a gruff and often shirtless man in his eighties, and quite rough around the edges, but something about him drew us in. Underneath the tough exterior, we started seeing glimpses of a hurting heart. I began to pray for him and for the opportunity to share Jesus. At his age, I knew time was not on his side, and I became so burdened for him to find peace with God. I often thought, *How in the world can I go around the country sharing about Jesus when my own next-door neighbor doesn't know Him?* I continued praying for a green light from the Lord to share my story with him.

One day Robb was out blowing leaves and looked over and saw Mr. Smith doing the same. So Robb, being such a fun-loving kid at heart, snuck up from behind and put his leaf blower up the back of Mr. Smith's unbuttoned shirt. Thankfully, they both got a big laugh out of it and, believe it or not, that crazy incident endeared us to his heart. From that point on, Mr. Smith would run outside whenever he saw us and talk to us for hours.

We stocked him up with my albums and even a concert video, so he quickly became acquainted with our ministry and found it very fascinating. He always wanted to know when and where we were going each weekend, and he often had the schedule memorized better than Robb.

Then, one day changed everything. 9/11. Mr. Smith knew we had been doing concerts and would be flying home from New England on that exact day. Obviously, with all of the terror and chaos, our flight out of New Hampshire was cancelled. It took an extra day to get home since we had to rent a car and drive down the East Coast to Virginia.

When we pulled into our driveway, Mr. Smith immediately ran out to greet us. For a moment, the gruff exterior was gone, and he quickly hugged us and told us how happy he was to see us. He said he had been so worried because he wasn't sure where we were flying in and out of, and he wasn't sure if we were okay.

As we stood there in our driveway discussing the horrifying tragedy, out of the blue, Mr. Smith looked us in the eye and said, "I guess I need to hurry up and figure out whether there's a God or not because I'm not getting any younger." It was as if God showed up and said to me, "Now is the time, Paula. Here's your green light."

I began to tell him my story and how God intervened and saved me. Mr. Smith listened with rapt attention to every word I said. However, at the end of my story, he shared his story, which included one of his sons being killed by a drunk driver. All these years he carried that pain and his heart echoed the question, *How could a good God allow bad things to happen?* It's a question that many have languished over throughout the course of time.

I went on to explain to Mr. Smith how we live in a fallen world where people make choices that have consequences. God does not make us robots, and He gives each of us a free will. Unfortunately, within that free will, people make sinful choices that affect not only their lives, but the lives of others as well.

From that point on, my heart broke for Mr. Smith. I began

praying for him every single day as I walked or drove past his house. I asked God to continue working in his heart and to show Mr. Smith his need for Jesus.

One night, we had Mr. Smith and his wife over for dinner. Robb and I decided beforehand that we wanted to keep it light and fun, but Mr. Smith had other plans. From the moment he walked into our house until the moment he left, all he wanted to do was ask questions and talk about God. When he left that night, he stopped on our porch and said, "If I ever become a Christian, it is going to be because of you people. But I don't think I ever will." My heart broke even more and tears filled my eyes as he and his wife walked away. I couldn't help but think of Acts 26:28 [KJV], where King Agrippa said to the Apostle Paul, "You almost persuaded me to become a Christian."

Months later, we invited Mr. Smith to a local concert I was performing at. We assured him he could just slip in the back and make himself at home to which he responded, "The back? If I'm going, I'm going to sit in the front row." And that's exactly what he did. At the end of the concert, the pastor got up and gave an invitation for people to receive Jesus. He even said in the invitation, "Maybe you have questions of how a good God could allow bad things to happen to you." I about fell over. *How did that pastor know to say that?* I fully expected Mr. Smith to respond, but he didn't.

Six months later, I was speaking at a ladies' conference in Alaska. During one of my sessions, I referred to Mr. Smith, and when I was finished speaking, the pastor's wife prayed for Jim

Smith to receive Christ. That night, while I was still in Alaska, I got a call from one of our neighbors. They shared with me that they had a Sunday school class pool party at their house that day and right in the middle of it Mr. Smith's son came over to the party and wanted to talk. To make a long story short, Mr. Smith's son prayed right then and there at the pool party and received Jesus as his Savior. I have to say I was very excited to think that while we were praying in Alaska, Jim Smith Jr. was praying and receiving Christ. I also had to laugh and ask, *Lord, do I really need to pray more specifically? We are praying for Jim Smith Sr. to come to know You!*

Our prayers continued for another year. Then, one quiet spring afternoon, the doorbell rang. It was Mr. Smith. We sat down on the porch with him as he quietly shared that even though he still had many questions he had finally prayed in the middle of the night to receive Jesus as his Savior. He finally took that step of faith. I didn't know whether to laugh or cry, and I think I did both! I thought my heart would just burst right open. I jumped right up and gave him a huge hug.

As I thought about it later, I had to laugh at how God works. It wasn't in the hours of talking in the driveway, it wasn't while having a meal at our home, and it wasn't even at my concert that Mr. Smith came to Jesus. No, it had nothing to do with my words or the opportunities I continuously tried to create; it was all about the still, small voice speaking life into his heart. Many people had already given up on Mr. Smith, but I am so thankful that no one is too hardened, too old, or too far from God's reach.

He can reach down and change anyone's heart if they will just take a step of faith and believe.

Maybe you have a Mr. Smith in your life—someone you have been lifting up in prayer for years to come to know Jesus. Don't give up! God works even when we don't know He is working. He can do the miraculous!

Maybe you have a situation or a dream you have prayed earnestly for and you're discouraged because you haven't seen any results. Keep praying and believing! Nothing is impossible with God.

Or maybe you are like Mr. Smith, full of questions and struggling to believe. You don't have to have it all together. You can come as you are and take a small step of faith to believe, and God will do the rest. It's never too late to change. It's never too late to come to Jesus. You have nothing to lose and everything to gain by beginning a relationship with your Creator. When you place your faith in Him, He will transform your life and take you beyond your wildest dreams!

Dream Weaving

Living out our dreams begins with having the faith to believe. If we don't have the faith to believe, then we will never get past the first challenge that comes our way. Faith is believing even when we can't see the road ahead or when life doesn't always make sense. This kind of unswerving faith is found when we firmly believe that God is in control and has our best interests at the center of His plan for our lives. Placing our absolute trust in Him allows God to do the miraculous, to revive our broken dreams, and to transform our lives through a vibrant relationship with Him. It only takes a step of faith to get started on the journey to living beyond our dreams, so why not take that step today?

Think of a time in your life when your faith wavered and you struggled with unbelief. How did you deal with it? Did it make you press into God or turn away from Him?

_____

_____

_____

_____

_____

_____

_____

_____

_____

_____

_____

_____

_____

What are some situations that you are currently trusting God with? Are you asking and believing Him for the miraculous? Write out each scenario. Be specific with your requests, thanking Him in advance for what He is going to do. When we thank Him in advance, we are not only recognizing that He CAN do the miraculous, but we are also anticipating and believing that He WILL work on our behalf.

_____

_____

_____

_____

_____

_____

_____

_____

_____

_____

_____

Look back in this chapter to the list from Psalm 37 describing trust. Go down that list and rate yourself on how you are actively living out each of these in your life. On a scale of 1 to 5, with 1 being very weak and 5 being very strong, how do you rate yourself in each area of trust? Ask the Lord to help you in the areas that you struggle with.

_____

_____

_____

_____

_____

_____

_____

_____

_____

_____

_____

_____

If you were to take an honest look at yourself, would you say that you go through the motions in your relationship with God? Are you more concerned about doing all the right things before Him or being right with Him. Take a moment and write a prayer to the Lord asking Him to rid you of anything that is not authentic and pleasing to Him, and ask Him to draw you into an intimate and growing relationship of love with Him.

_____

_____

_____

_____

_____

_____

_____

_____

_____

_____

_____

Are there any ways that you are currently playing it safe with your dreams? What are you actively doing that can only be accomplished if God intervenes? What would you do if you knew it would succeed? Search your heart. Dream God-sized dreams. Take some time and journal, asking God to do what only He can do in and through you.

_____

_____

_____

_____

_____

_____

_____

_____

_____

_____

_____

_____

_____

Are you praying for someone who needs Jesus? Maybe you have been praying for years, even decades. Don't give up. Keep praying and believing for a miracle, for no one's heart is too far from God's reach. Take a moment and list out each person you are burdened for. Write out a prayer in the space below, asking God to break through the walls of unbelief and to soften their searching heart with the love and hope of Jesus Christ.

_____

_____

_____

_____

_____

_____

_____

_____

_____

_____

_____

_____

_____

Have you experienced saving faith? Or are you allowing doubts and questions to hold you back? You have absolutely nothing to lose and everything to gain. Take that step of faith to believe, and God will do the rest. If you don't know Jesus, you can pray right now in the quietness of your heart something like this:

"Jesus, I know I'm a sinner (Romans 3:23). I believe that You came and died on the cross to pay for my sin (Romans 6:23, John 3:16). Please forgive me and come into my life to be my Lord and Savior (Romans 10:13). Thank You for this gift of salvation. Help me to live for You from this day forward."

If you prayed this prayer, I would love to celebrate with you. You can email me at pauladunnministries.com. Once you begin a relationship with Jesus, it is so important that you grow in your faith through reading His Word and in prayer. Also, finding a Bible-believing church is so important to encourage you, to strengthen you, and to teach you as you begin this exciting journey of faith. The Bible says that all of Heaven rejoices when one person receives Christ. So I just know there is a party going on in Heaven right now for YOU!

Chapter 8

The Road Less Traveled

DON'T WE ALL WISH THERE WAS A CUT-AND-DRIED formula that we could implement in our lives to guarantee success? While such a list clearly doesn't exist, there are some life principles that, if taken seriously, do position us for greater potential in reaching our dreams. I would like to share a list with you of ten life principles that have made a huge difference in my own life. While this is not an exhaustive list, I do believe it covers some of the most important components of success in the pursuit of our dreams.

#1 PRAY WITH POWER

I know this sounds very basic, but I believe it is often when we overlook the basics that we can get a little sloppy in our day-to-day lives. Praying with power is so much more than just throwing up a quick prayer over a meal or at bedtime. Praying with power starts with emptying ourselves of us and asking God to fill us with Him. It is getting out of the way so God can show up and take over.

I learned this lesson first-hand on another concert road trip Robb and I took as a newly married couple. We were especially excited to have a concert within a few hours from home. So, we got up early Sunday morning and headed out. Once we were about halfway there, I decided to use the rest of the time in the car to prepare for the concert. I began to pray specifically asking God to anoint the service and to draw the people there who needed Jesus. About an hour later, we arrived at the church and immediately set up for the concert, did a sound check, and then it was time to begin.

Right from the start, I knew people were hurting. When it came time for the invitation, the altars were packed with people praying to receive Jesus and others praying to surrender their lives to Him. It was such a powerful service, and we were so thrilled to be a part of it. When it was all over, there was a young man still kneeling at the altar. We went over to talk to him and found out that he had just prayed to accept Jesus as his Savior. Here's the best part: just that morning, at 9:30 a.m. (right about the exact time when I was praying in the car), he had been released from jail. He went on to tell us that he had nowhere to go and nowhere to turn and felt DRAWN to that particular church that morning. I could hardly contain myself. We had prayed in the car right around that exact time that God would DRAW people who needed to be at this service. Talk about answered prayer!

Later, as I thought about the events of that concert, I realized that my previous prayers were more often along the lines of asking the Lord to give me the words to say or to help my voice to be strong, but I realized that day that it is not about me at all. It is not about my words, my voice, or my songs; it is all about the Holy Spirit working, drawing, and changing people's hearts. This lesson truly revolutionized our concerts from that day forward. We now see many decisions for Christ on a regular basis, and I believe it is because the focus is no longer on me but on those who need Jesus.

If we will learn to pray with power, God will honor those prayers and do a mighty work in our hearts, in our dreams, and in the lives of those around us.

#2 PRACTICE PATIENCE

Isaiah 40:31 tells us that those who wait on the Lord will renew their strength. This can be very difficult for me because I want to reach my goals yesterday, and sometimes God's timing can be very different from my own. If I am not careful, I can plunge ahead of God when I think He is not working fast enough in my life. The problem with plunging ahead of God is that it takes me out of the realm of walking with Him and into the territory of walking on my own, pursuing my own plans, and going in my own strength. That is why it is so important to understand that God's ways and His timing are not always identical to ours, and the only way to figure out what our response should be in a given situation is to get on our knees before Him and bathe everything we do in prayer.

There are two extremes to this, however. While plunging ahead of God can sometimes be my tendency, the other extreme is remaining in a holding pattern while "waiting on God." We all have heard people say, "I'm just waiting on God to show me what to do with my life." Meanwhile, years go by and they never attempt anything. Both extremes require us to do our part and ask God for direction and clarity moving forward.

Because I know my tendency is to speed forward as if everything is a green light, my prayer needs to be for God to stop me dead in my tracks when the light is red. Those who see all opportunities as a red light need to ask God to make it very clear what He wants them to do and to push them forward when they have a green light.

Waiting can be very hard, but it is during these waiting times that God can draw us to Himself, mold us, and prepare us for what He has right around the corner. The waiting time is a preparation time. Therefore, it is important that we see it as such and use it to prepare ourselves for the awesome opportunities that lie ahead.

#3 PLAN FOR MISTAKES

Let's face it; no matter how hard we try, no one is perfect, and that is a hard pill to swallow for those of us who are perfectionists and overachievers. I think motherhood most definitely has given me opportunities for mistakes despite all the effort on my part to do otherwise.

When I became pregnant with my daughter Emma, only on rare occasions would you see me without my nose stuck in the book *What to Expect When You're Expecting,* and I think I even had the book *Babywise* just about memorized. I was determined to be the best mom that I could be, but Emma was anything but textbook—starting with the emergency C-section and most definitely including the seven or eight wakings every night until she was three due to severe reflux. I quickly learned that all the preparing and reading I had done ahead of time was pretty much for nothing because I had absolutely no idea what I was doing.

Perhaps one of the worst mommy-fail moments was on a concert weekend when we took Emma with us. Thankfully, my sweet mother-in-law came along to help. On the way home, Emma was very fussy. Nothing would pacify her. I tried feeding her throughout the day, but all she would do was cry. I became worried that she was ill and even gave her Tylenol to help her feel better. To make a long story short, at the end of the day my mother-in-law figured out that her bottle was clogged. I felt so terrible! The poor little thing was starving and once she had an unclogged bottle she sure guzzled it for all she was worth!

Then, there's the time she was sick with a really bad cold. We had a vaporizer going in her bedroom to help with all the congestion. About forty minutes after laying her down for her nap, Robb and I both went in to check on her. As we approached her bedroom, all we could see was steam pouring out from under her door. Robb quickly opened the door to find that the steam was so thick we literally couldn't even see her crib. I don't know if it was from my lack of sleep or my overzealousness in wanting to help her stuffy nose, but when I laid Emma down for her nap I guess I got a little crazy with the salt in the vaporizer. Let's just say her hair was very curly and her skin was very hydrated after that nap!

We still laugh about both stories today, and yes, I still get teased about them. My point is that no matter how hard we try, we will never be perfect. Attempting to be perfect at everything only leads to disappointment, frustration, and might stop us before we even get started in pursuing our dreams. It's important to realize that the only perfect person is Jesus, so take the pressure off and allow room for mistakes.

I have found the best way not to take ourselves so seriously is learning to laugh at ourselves. Not only does it take the pressure off, but it can also make for great laughs with family and friends and can provide some free therapy. After all, Proverbs 17:22 [KJV] does say, "A merry heart does good, like medicine."

#4 PICK YOUR FRIENDS AND MENTORS WISELY

As iron sharpens iron, so a man sharpens the countenance of his friend.
—Proverbs 27:17 KJV

While we all can have a large number of acquaintances in our lives, the people we trust with our hopes and dreams need to be a select few—those who will be honest yet loving, who want the best for us, and who will cheer us on.

Who are your closest friends? Can you say that you are a better person because of the time spent with them? Do they point you to Jesus or pull you away from Him? Do they challenge you to be a better spouse, parent, and friend? Is it a healthy friendship with a good balance of give and take? These are all great questions to ask yourself about each close friendship. The answers might surprise you.

After reflecting on my own relationships, I have found that some friendships weren't as strong as I thought they were once I really took a closer look. This is an important distinction because we only have a certain amount of time available to pour into friendships. I want to make sure I am choosing the right friendships. I want to invest in friendships that sharpen me and spur me on to live the dreams God has for me.

#5 PURSUE INTEGRITY

What is integrity? Webster defines it as "adherence to a code of values, utter sincerity, honesty, and candor."[15] While honesty definitely is the foundation of integrity, I'd like to break it down to bare bones by saying integrity is who we are when no one is watching. It's easy to feign honesty when people are looking, but the real test of character is when there is no one around.

What do you do when you realize the store clerk gave you twenty dollars back instead of one? Or how about the temptation to skew the truth to protect ourselves from looking bad when we have had a second fender bender in just two months (yes, I'm referring to myself)? While these may seem small and insignificant, if we can't be honest and show integrity in the small things, we will eventually struggle with the big things. There is someone who is always watching. God sees everything and He even knows the motives of our hearts. (See Proverbs 17:3b.)

Integrity is who we are when no one is watching.

Psalm 101 is a vow of integrity written by David that includes the following:

- I will pay attention to the way of integrity.
- I will live with integrity of heart in my house.
- I will not set anything godless before my eyes.
- I hate the doing of transgression; it will not cling to me.
- A devious heart will be far from me; I will not be involved with evil.
- No one who acts deceitfully will live in my palace.
- No one who tells lies will remain in my presence.

This is a great vow to implement in our families, in our friendships, in our careers, and most importantly with our God. What really stands the test of time is our character and our integrity, and both have a huge impact in whether we succeed or fail in reaching our dreams.

#6 PERSIST WITH EXCELLENCE

Whatever your hands find to do, do it with all your strength.
—Ecclesiastes 9:10 HCSB

In the pursuit of success, there are no shortcuts when it comes to giving your all. Notice the verse above says, "all your strength." I believe when we allow ourselves to slip into halfheartedness, it shows that we are not fully committed to achieving our dreams. It takes an unwavering and sold-out commitment to excellence to be successful. Excellence should be a given to anything we invest ourselves in because not only does it have our name on it, but if we are followers of Christ, it bears His name as well. Thus, there is no room for laziness. To be successful takes our all.

We also need to take notice of the first part of Ecclesiastes 9:10, "Whatever your hands find to do…." It's easy to give our all to the things we enjoy and skip over the things we don't, but that will not get us ahead in life. Shortcuts rarely pay off and often require us doing tasks over and over, putting us further behind than when we started. Whatever your hands find to do, whether cleaning toilets, changing diapers, mowing lawns, fixing meals, or working in corporate America, all the menial daily tasks can be done with or without excellence. The choice is up to us—a choice that may seem trivial, but a choice that defines the essence of who we are.

I have shared with you about the camp that gave me my start with singing. In addition to my singing responsibilities, I was also given the job of cleaning the girl's bathroom each day. Have you ever cleaned a bathroom shared by 100 or more teenage girls? Let's just say it was far from glamorous! I remember mopping the bathroom floor one day singing, "Humble thyself in the sight of the Lord, and He will lift you up" (James 4:10 KJV). It was definitely a lesson in humility, but here's what I learned: If we will be faithful in the small, thankless tasks in life, then we can be trusted with the larger ones down the road. When we give our all to even the unglamorous, it shows we are committed to excellence in whatever we do and we will not accept anything less than our best, which is a key trait of champions.

If we will be faithful in the small, thankless tasks in life, then we can be trusted with the larger ones down the road.

#7 PRIORITIZE YOUR COMMITMENTS

In order to prioritize our commitments, we must first establish our priorities and commitments. A great exercise to discover where our priorities lie is to sit down and account for how we spend each of our 168 hours in a week. Lysa TerKeurst talks about this in her book *The Best Yes*.[16] It is so revealing when we actually dissect how we spend our time, for it definitely highlights how we can waste our time on frivolous things.

If we want to be successful, we must know our purpose, our abilities, our priorities, and when to say no. This quandary of what to say yes to and what to say no to can be a struggle for me because I often attempt to take on everything, creating an abyss of exhaustion, frustration, and mediocre efforts at best because I'm spread too thin.

As I juggle being a wife, mom, and traveling with my ministry, I have learned to be more intentional with what I say yes to, for when I say yes to everything I am often saying no to Robb and Emma. Not that everything I do must be about them, but it certainly should be done with careful consideration of them. Saying yes to everything is not healthy for my family or my well-being. That is why it is so important to pray through our commitments and to be intentional.

When I say yes to everything, I am often saying no to my family.

#8 PAY IT FORWARD

Paying it forward involves two basic principles. The first is being grateful for where you are, and the second is, out of that gratefulness, blessing others as you move forward. For every milestone of success in life, there are people who help us along the way—people who believe in us, give us a chance, and cheer us on. It is so important to take the time to show gratefulness to those who have played a part in our lives.

Luke 17 tells the story of the ten lepers. As Jesus entered a village, He was met by ten men with a serious skin disease. They watched from afar and begged Jesus to have mercy and heal them. Jesus told them to go to the priest and show themselves, and as they went they were healed. After the fact, when they each saw that they were healed, only one returned to thank Jesus and give Him the glory.

Wow. I can't imagine being healed from such a miserable disease and not thanking the One who healed me. Yet, when we get too busy and do not choose to show our thankfulness to God and to those around us, we are just as the other nine lepers whose hearts were self-absorbed rather than grateful. Gratefulness is a choice of the heart, a choice to recognize and give thanks for acts of kindness and deeds of love by those around us.

However, it doesn't stop there. A truly grateful person can't help but bless others because of how deeply they have been so blessed. For example, when my husband first started investing in real estate there were people who gave him a chance and owner-financed some properties to him, which paved the way for him to get started and do what he loved to do. Robb has worked hard and God has blessed him with over 300 properties in fifteen years, and I can honestly say that nothing brings Robb more joy than helping other young investors get started and creating deals to help them do so. You see, a grateful heart often leads to a generous heart.

A grateful heart often leads to a generous heart.

In Proverbs 3:27, the Bible talks about not withholding good when it is in your power. Imagine if we all decided to do good to those around us whenever it was in our power to do so—think of the impact that would have on our families, our neighborhoods, our communities, and even our world.

#9 PARTY WHEN YOU MEET A GOAL

The pursuit of our dreams often requires long hours, hard work, and unrelenting resolve. That is why it is so important to acknowledge each milestone of accomplishment. In essence, life can't be just about working hard and reaching goals; part of the journey is celebrating along the way. I must admit that Robb and I love celebrating each other in this way.

When I was finishing up my Master's Degree in counseling, I was truly burning the candle at both ends as I studied for comprehensive exams, counseled and filed reports for my internship, and traveled and sang every weekend. It was exhausting, but I knew it would only be insanely crazy like that for a year. I can't even begin to tell you how relieved and elated I was to graduate.

When I came home after completing the last comprehensive test and after turning in the last of my course work, there was a beautifully wrapped package waiting for me. I eagerly opened it and found a sweet note from my husband telling me how proud he was of me along with a brand new bathing suit with a note attached saying we were headed to Florida for some much needed rest and relaxation. That trip meant the world to me because it symbolized a major milestone in my journey. Likewise, whenever Robb has closed on his real estate investment deals, we have always gone to a nice restaurant to celebrate because there is nothing sweeter than enjoying the benefits of hard work and diligence with those we love. So, when you have worked hard to reach a goal, don't miss out on the best part of all, celebrating your hard work and God's blessings with those you love.

#10 PERSEVERE FOR THE LONG HAUL

Nothing takes the place of determination and sticking with your dream no matter the cost. You have to stay at it when you're up and when you're down. You must stick it out whether you feel like it or not. Let's face it, there are days when we don't feel like pursuing our dreams, but we must not fall into the trap of allowing our feelings to be our guide. Feelings come and go, and feelings change. Therefore, it is commitment that we must go on in order to be successful.

While a student at Liberty University, Dr. Falwell would

often challenge us not to quit. At the beginning of the semester, when the workload was kicking in, and then during finals week, when we could barely keep our heads above water, he would always read this poem:

Don't Quit

When things go wrong, as they sometimes will,
When the road you're trudging seems uphill,
When funds are low, and the debts are high,
And you want to smile, but you have to sigh,
When care is pressing you down a bit,
Rest if you must, but don't quit.

Life is odd with its twists and turns,
As every one of us sometimes learns,
And many a failure turns about,
When he might have won had he stuck it out.
Don't give up though the pace seems slow,
You may succeed with another blow.

Success is failure turned inside out,
The silver tint of the clouds of doubt,
And you never can tell how close you are,
It may be near when it seems so far.
So stick in the fight when you're hardest hit,
It's when things seem worst that you must not quit.

—Author Unknown

Maybe you are reading this and you have been struggling with wanting to quit. We all have those moments in our lives, but I want to encourage you not to give in to that feeling. Make the commitment today to persevere for the long haul and never quit! You will never regret persevering toward your dreams.

Dream Weaving

The road to success is often marked with good intentions, but in order to reach our dreams we must replace good intentions with commitment. Commitment to integrity, excellence, and perseverance are just a few of the fundamental life principles that can take us from mediocrity to extraordinary living. While adherence to these principles doesn't guarantee success, it certainly gives us greater potential for rising above our greatest obstacles and living beyond our wildest dreams.

How do you approach praying for your dreams? Do you take the time to list your requests? Do you ask God to show up and take over in each situation? On a scale of 1 to 10, how do you rate your prayers (with 1 being weak and ineffective and 10 being full of power)? Dr. Falwell always preached that nothing of eternal significance is accomplished apart from prayer. Determine today to pray with power.

_____

_____

_____

_____

_____

_____

_____

_____

_____

_____

_____

_____

What are you waiting on God for? How do you see Him molding you in the process? Do you ever run ahead of God? List some areas where you are seeking His direction, and ask Him to either make it very clear whether you should proceed or to stop you in your tracks.

_____

_____

_____

_____

_____

_____

_____

_____

_____

_____

_____

_____

_____

_____

Can you laugh at your mistakes? Think of a mistake you have made in your life and then find some humor in it. You might be surprised how good it feels to laugh at yourself.

_____

_____

_____

_____

_____

_____

_____

_____

_____

_____

_____

_____

_____

_____

Who are your inner-circle friends? Do they tell you the truth in love, want the best for you, and cheer you on? Do your friendships have a healthy balance of give and take? Take time this week to evaluate your close friendships. Also, what kind of friend are you? Do you take the time to invest in your friends' lives and build them up? Look for opportunities this week to speak an encouraging word or to do something special for those closest to you.

_____

_____

_____

_____

_____

_____

_____

_____

_____

_____

_____

_____

Can you honestly say that you are living a life of integrity? Do you strive to be a person of character at all times, not just when people are around? Write out Psalm 15 in the space provided and think about these verses this week as you go about your day-to-day activities. Strive to show integrity in everything you do and say.

_____

_____

_____

_____

_____

_____

_____

_____

_____

_____

_____

_____

_____

Do you pursue excellence in all that you do? How about in the thankless, menial, daily tasks? What are some areas you could improve on in giving your all?

_____

_____

_____

_____

_____

_____

_____

_____

_____

_____

_____

_____

_____

_____

_____

_____

List your top priorities in order. Then, categorize where the hours of your week are spent. How much time do you devote to your priorities? Are you spending time on things that aren't important? Pray through each commitment, being intentional in what gets a yes. Make sure your commitments align with your familial responsibilities and what God has called you to do. If you need to eliminate something, don't wait another day. Find the courage to say no and focus on where God is directing you.

_____

_____

_____

_____

_____

_____

_____

_____

_____

_____

_____

_____

Do you take the time to celebrate when you or a loved one reaches an important goal? When was the last time you did so? Take a moment and jot down some ideas for celebrating accomplishments with those you love. Make a commitment now to be a family that celebrates when one of you succeeds.

_____

_____

_____

_____

_____

_____

_____

_____

_____

_____

_____

_____

_____

_____

_____

_____

Have you ever felt like giving up on something? Maybe you are currently in a situation that makes you want to quit. If so, use the space below to write a prayer to the Lord, asking Him for strength and renewed hope in persevering for the long haul. Ask Him for the endurance to run the race that is set before you, as found in Hebrews 12:1, and to finish strong.

_____

_____

_____

_____

_____

_____

_____

_____

_____

_____

_____

_____

_____

_____

Chapter 9

The Time Is Now

AS I TRAVEL AND SPEAK TO DIFFERENT WOMEN'S groups, one of my favorite topics to talk about is time because it is something every single one of us can relate to. It doesn't matter how old or young you may be, and it doesn't matter what season of life you are in, we all have the same twenty-four hours in a day. However, it's how we spend those twenty-four hours that varies so drastically and reveals what is important to each of us.

As we discussed in the last chapter, if you want to see what matters to someone, examine how they spend their time. This is important because how we spend our time directly affects how we spend our lives. When we struggle with how to spend our time, it is often because we have lost sight of why we are here on this earth, what our purpose is, and of the dreams God has called us to live out. Once we have our purpose firmly nailed down, it is so much easier to know how to spend our time.

HAVE A PLAN

In addition to knowing our purpose, we must also have a plan in order to manage our lives effectively. I don't think any of us would set out for a coast-to-coast road trip without some sort of directions. If you're a high-tech person, I bet you are just chomping at the bit to pull out your GPS system or to set up your iPhone or iPad Maps App at just the mere mention of a trip. That would be my husband. Don't tell him I told you, but I have even seen him type in an address when he already knew the directions just for the sheer fun of seeing it on his iPad. I, on the other hand, am a good old-fashioned paper-map girl. I like to have the entire atlas in front of me so I can see all the states and even look them up individually if I so choose without the worry of hitting a wrong button and the whole thing disappearing.

Regardless of what mapping system you prefer, I'm sure we can all agree that directions are essential for navigating our way through unknown territory. Yet, how many times do we go through life without a plan or any forethought regarding our future? This is where goals are so important in keeping us focused and using our time to propel us toward our dreams. The times we go adrift in life can often be attributed to not taking the time to set goals and not planning for the future.

Robb and I start every year off with a goal-setting date in January. We pick our favorite restaurant and spend the evening looking at our goals. We start by looking at last year's goals to see how we measured up. While it is definitely fun to see the progress, it also is motivating to assess the goals that were not reached and to redefine them if necessary. We then look at the upcoming year and carve out new goals for our marriage, for parenting, for our ministry, for our careers, and for us as individuals. Once this has been completed, we finish up by discussing our long-term goals. I have to say, this not only creates a great plan of action, but it also unifies us as a couple as we work together to reach our goals for our future.

SET GOALS

It has been said that goals are dreams with deadlines. If we want to live out the dreams God has called us to, we must be diligent in not only making a plan, but also in setting a deadline that gives us accountability and forces us to move forward. When was the last time you set some deadlines for your dreams? Below are a few principles to help you get started.

To move beyond where you are currently at in life, you must set goals that challenge and stretch you.

- Goals should be an extension of your dream. Also, make sure they coincide with your priorities.
- Goals should be specific. If you are vague, it gives you a way out; therefore, be as detailed as possible in defining

your goals.

- Goals should be measurable. Be specific about when you want to see each goal met.
- Goals need to be written down. I once read that a thought-about goal is a wish, whereas a written-about goal becomes a commitment.

How we live our days is how we live our lives.

—Annie Dillard

I love this quote by Annie Dillard: "How we live our days is how we live our lives." When we waste time, we are wasting life. In this sense, our daily routines really do matter. I know that sounds very black and white, but it is so true. I cannot emphasize enough the importance of making a daily to-do list. I remember hearing in youth group as a teenager that if you aim at nothing, you will hit it every time, and so it is with planning our days. It's important to have a to-do list not only to keep us on track, but also to point us in the right direction when those unexpected free moments open up in our schedules. Rather than running in circles trying to figure out what we need to do next, a to-do list has it already spelled out right in front of us.

Creating a to-do list can be as simple as jotting down a list of tasks that must be accomplished within that day in a Day-Timer, notebook, or even on a whiteboard on the wall. Some people like to prioritize their daily tasks by labeling them A for most urgent, B for important, and C for something that may not be pressing but eventually needs to be done (Franklin Covey is a system that teaches this ABC approach). Once we accomplish a task, we can check it off (which is one of my favorite things to do), and the tasks that are not accomplished can be carried over to the next day. While there is nothing magical about writing out our tasks, having each task listed in front of us each day gives us a much greater chance of following through, which in turn can give us greater success in reaching our dreams and goals.

ELIMINATE TIME WASTERS

Looking for and eliminating time wasters is also an important way to maximize our time. Television, Facebook, Pinterest, Twitter, and surfing the net are just a few of the time-wasting traps we can get lured into if we are not careful. It's not that we can never relax or do anything that is not productive. Sometimes we need to take a break to renew ourselves. As with anything in life, balance is the key, and one way to know if you are balanced or not is to honestly assess yourself on how you spend your time each day. What activities encompass your day and how much time do you spend doing them? We figure this out when we examine exactly how we spend the twenty-four hours that we have in each day. Taking an inside look at our day not only helps us quickly recognize if we are balanced, but it also reveals the activities that may need to be adjusted in order to be more productive with our time.

STICK TO THE TASK

In order to stay focused on our goals, we must guard against bunny trails and stick to the task at hand. Here's an example: You know you have company arriving in four short hours, so you ferociously dive into cleaning your house. As you go to pull out your cleaning supplies, you notice the linen closet needs a good overhaul. Since you are already in cleaning mode, you begin to pull everything out. While doing so, you remember that you need to take some meat out of the freezer to thaw out for the dinner you will be preparing. So you quickly race to the kitchen to grab the meat, and you are overcome by the rancid smell mysteriously permeating throughout your kitchen. In an effort to find the source, you begin to clean out the refrigerator, take out the trash, and organize your pantry.

I think you get my point. I have learned that if I don't practice discipline in carrying out my goals, I can end up all over the place and further behind than when I started.

But the game changer for me is people. I don't want to be so busy checking off my to-do list and focusing on my tasks that I miss out on people God has placed in my path for a reason. Maybe it's just for a quick hug and a friendly hello or maybe it's to sit down and listen and offer hope. People are always more important than tasks.

If you look at the life of Jesus, you will see that He always took time for people. It didn't matter how tired He was or if He had already spent a full day ministering—He loved people. When we begin our day asking God to use us, He will set up divine appointments for us to be a shining light to those around us. We must be looking for the opportunities and be willing to take the time to touch a life.

START YOUR DAY WITH GOD

The most important thing we can do to maximize our day is to start our day off with God. Spending time with Him in prayer and reading His Word strengthens us and prepares our minds and our hearts for every opportunity we encounter. Make an appointment with Him. I know that sounds so cut-and-dried, but if we don't have a set time, it usually won't happen. We make appointments for everything that matters to us—haircuts, manicures, workouts, yearly checkups, dental appointments, car repairs, and the list goes on, so why not make an appointment with God?

Whenever I am on the road without Robb and Emma, I can tell you right now that I make time to talk to them. I can't wait to hear their voices, and now I especially enjoy seeing their sweet faces with Facetime. Often, we will talk several times throughout the day because I don't want to miss out on anything in their lives. Even though it can be so loud and obnoxious trying to talk to them while running through airports, I would never let a day or two go by without being a part of their lives. Yet how many times do I let a day or two go by without spending quality time with Jesus? And He's the most important person of all. We say we love Him, but what does our time spent with Him say? If we want to see Jesus' power in our lives, we must begin each day by spending time with Him.

SEE EACH DAY AS A GIFT

God has given every one of us the gift of time each day. What we do with that time is our gift back to Him. Right now, as I am typing, it is 10:00 a.m., which means almost half of my day is gone—hours that I can never relive again. What have I done with these hours? Can I say that I have spent any of that time in a meaningful way? Imagine if we looked at every hour of each day through the lens of eternity. I have a feeling we would live a little differently—perhaps more intentionally.

Activity is not necessarily accomplishment.
—John Maxwell

Psalm 90:12&14b [NKJV] says, "Teach us [Lord] to number our days.... That we may rejoice and be glad all our days!" Then in James 4:14 it says that our lives are vapors that appear for a short while and then quickly vanish away. I couldn't agree more. It feels like just yesterday I was a teenager and somehow I blinked and now I'm in my 40s. Life is just flying by. That is why it is so important to know our purpose, to have a plan, and to live every moment passionately with everything we have inside.

We all know how to be busy and run around from sun up to sun down, but what are we really accomplishing? John Maxwell profoundly says, "Activity is not necessarily accomplishment."[17] I don't want to just be busy. I want to live my life for things that matter, things that will last beyond my life here on Earth. Tim Kizzair sums it up best by saying, "Our greatest fear should not be of failure but of succeeding at things that don't really matter."[18] I want to make a difference, and I don't want to have a single regret.

Our greatest fear should not be of failure but of succeeding at things that don't really matter.

—Tim Kizzair

LIVE A LIFE OF NO REGRETS

Years ago I received a phone call from my brother informing me that my biological father had been rushed to the hospital. He experienced a heart attack and a stroke and was not expected to live. I quickly boarded an airplane and headed to Maine to be with my family. As I entered the hospital room and saw my dad lying there in the bed that day, I began to think of his life and saw a little boy who had come from a broken home in an era when divorce was not as acceptable as it is today. I remembered the story he often told of himself as an eager kid waiting at the door all day long for a promised fishing trip with his dad that never took place. I saw him as a man who struggled with knowing how to give and receive love his whole life. And most of all, I looked and saw my dad with a heart full of pain and a lifetime of regret. I leaned in and quietly told him he didn't have to have any regrets in life regarding me because he had truly given me the greatest gift of all by allowing a family to love me as their own and to share Jesus with me. I reminded him that, despite the demons of his past, he had placed his faith in Jesus and could rest assured that he would spend eternity with Him. I sang by his bedside until the wee hours of morning. I didn't know if he heard a single word I spoke or a single note I sang, but I knew I was right where I was supposed to be for that moment in time.

Throughout the visit, I felt a growing resolve from deep within me, a vow if you will, that I don't want to be at the end of my life with any regrets. I don't want to wish that I had done things differently.

Mistakes don't have to end up as regrets!

The good news is that we don't have to have any regrets. Every day is truly a new beginning and a clean slate to write our stories on. Mistakes don't have to end up as regrets. God can turn them around for His glory and His Kingdom and make something beautiful out of it. The choice is up to us. Do you want to make a difference with your life and invest in things that matter? Do you want to make every moment count? Here's an excerpt from a commencement address by Mark Batterson that beautifully sums up a life filled with purpose and without regret:

Quit living as if the purpose of life is to arrive safely at death. Set God-sized goals. Pursue God-ordained passions. Go after a dream that is destined to fail without divine intervention. Keep asking questions. Keep making mistakes. Keep seeking God. Stop pointing out problems and become part of the solution. Stop repeating the past and start creating the future. Stop playing it safe and start taking risks. Expand your horizons. Accumulate experiences. Enjoy the journey. Find every excuse you can to celebrate everything you can. Live like today is the first day and last day of your life. Don't let what's wrong with you keep you from worshiping what's right with God. Burn sinful bridges. Blaze new trails. Don't let fear dictate your decisions. Take a flying leap of faith. Quit holding out. Quit holding back. Go all in with God. Go all out for God.[19]

Dream Weaving

We all have the same twenty-four hours each day, but how we spend those hours varies and ultimately comes down to what really matters to each of us. In order to make the most of our time here on this earth, we must have a plan which involves setting goals, eliminating time wasters, sticking to our tasks, and beginning each day by asking God to direct our steps. We only get one shot at this thing called life. Let's make sure we make every moment count so we will not find ourselves looking back at a lifetime of regrets one day.

Have you ever set goals for your life? Take time this week to write or review your goals for the different areas of your life—your marriage, parenting, ministry, career, and personal life. Don't forget to be specific. Set deadlines for each goal.

_____

_____

_____

_____

_____

_____

_____

_____

_____

_____

_____

_____

_____

_____

_____

Track how you spend your time each day this week. Here are some categories to help you get started: sleeping, time with God, time with family, time with friends, work, household responsibilities, exercise, ministry, errands, entertainment, etc. What are some time wasters you need to be careful with?

_____

_____

_____

_____

_____

_____

_____

_____

_____

_____

_____

_____

_____

_____

Do you allow for divine appointments to interrupt your day? Think of a time when a chance meeting turned into a divine encounter? Write a prayer to the Lord asking Him to direct your time, your steps, and your heart to those in need.

_____

_____

_____

_____

_____

_____

_____

_____

_____

_____

_____

_____

_____

_____

Do you see each day as a gift from God? Each hour as something you will never have again? Ask the Lord to help you live with intention and surrender—making the most of every moment as a gift back to Him.

_____

_____

_____

_____

_____

_____

_____

_____

_____

_____

_____

_____

_____

_____

_____

If you were suddenly at the end of your life, would you have any regrets? Would you wish you had done things differently? Maybe it's a relationship that needs mending. Maybe it's an opportunity you have never pursued. Only you can answer this question. Take time to search your heart and journal what comes to mind. Don't let another day go by without turning regret into a new beginning.

_____

_____

_____

_____

_____

_____

_____

_____

_____

_____

_____

_____

Chapter 10

Just Do It

THERE COMES A TIME IN LIFE WHEN WE HAVE TO quit talking about it, quit dreaming about it, quit thinking about it, and simply do it! That idea that races around in your head, keeping you awake at night—just do it! That dream that makes your heart practically pound out of your chest at the mere thought of it—just do it! That crazy venture that you know will cause you to fall flat on your face without God's intervention—just do it!

You will never know until you try. So why not join the Everest climbers and head for the summit of your dream? Why not be like Joshua and Caleb and see the potential of your promised land? The journey ahead to living your dream starts with taking that very first step.

TAKE THE FIRST STEP

Writing this book has been one of my dreams for many years. In the secret place of my heart, I knew that God had birthed a story in my life that He wanted me to share with as many people as possible. Throughout my ministry, when I've been asked about writing a book, I always said, "Someday, I'll write my story. It's just not the right time." However, if I'm honest, it wasn't just the timing that was holding me back. My perfectionism, fear of being out of my comfort zone, and the thought of pouring my whole heart out on paper scared me to death, but God kept chipping away at my fears.

Just this past summer, I attended a speaking and writing conference where I was challenged to pursue the "Best Yes" in my life. It wasn't in the keynote address or in a breakout workshop; it was in the quiet moments alone with God in my hotel room that I knew I was supposed to go home and write my story.

I pictured many months of staring at my computer desperately trying to work through writer's block. I wondered if midway I would be ready to call it quits and give up on this crazy dream of writing my story. But I have to tell you it has been anything but that. From the moment I typed the first word to this moment of concluding the final chapter, God has written my story. It has poured out of me so fast and furious that I have barely been able to keep up with it. I go to bed at night and I can hardly sleep because of my excitement to get up and continue my story—

years of traveling and singing and speaking all leading up to this very moment in time. I am in awe of God and how He works, how He prepares, and how He writes the story of our lives.

He is writing your story too. Like me, you may have fears that hold you back from getting started, but with God's help you can do this! Get on your knees and pray, take a deep breath, and then just dive right in. Let me be that Christian cheerleader in your life by saying, "Just do it!" Don't let your fears hold you back from realizing your dream! It's worth the risk and it's part of your journey.

John Maxwell gives the following statistics in his book *Your Bridge to a Better Future*:

- 40% of all people we come in contact with have good ideas but little or no motivation to make them happen;
- Another 40% attempt to make their ideas reality, but they don't see beyond their current circumstances;
- The last 20% have a dream and the ability to see that dream through to completion. There is no guarantee that this 20% will succeed, but they are more likely to do so than the 80% that don't dare to dream.[20]

I don't know about you, but I don't want to be a part of the 80% who miss out on living their dreams. I just can't sit around and talk about it. I have to do it! What is it you have to do? What will not leave you alone and what keeps speaking to your heart? What dream has God been preparing you for?

DARE TO LIVE YOUR DREAM

I want to leave you with a song I wrote years ago to perform at a National Amway Convention. It was written to inspire the audience to dare to dream. Over the years, however, it has become much more than a song to me; it has become an anthem of my heart. I pray that it can become an anthem of your heart as well. Go dream those dreams. Spread your wings. It's time to find the courage to rise above your circumstances, to live beyond your wildest dreams! So don't wait another moment—just do it!

Dare to Dream

There's a dream that's in you
and a dream that's in me.
A dream to make a difference
and be all that we can be.

There's a road that shines before us
if we will only see.
That the power of our dreams
can change our destiny.

Dare to dream. Dare to fly. Take a chance.
Don't let life pass you by.
There's a world that's waiting for you
if you will only try.
Dare to dream. Dare to fly.

There's a choice that you have of who you want to be.
A choice to touch a soul and to leave a legacy.
But it takes courage to step out and strength to lead the way.
So put your fears aside and realize that's why we're here today.

Dare to dream. Dare to fly. Take a chance.
Don't let life pass you by.
There's a world that's waiting for you if you will only try.
Dare to dream. Dare to fly.

God wants to use you, and He will see you through.
You'll see your life in a new light. The choice is up to you!

Dare to dream. Dare to fly. Take a chance.
Don't let life pass you by.
There's a world that's waiting for you if you will only try.
Dare to dream. Dare to fly.[21]

Dream Weaving

Taking the first steps toward our dreams is often the hardest part. If we will just throw our inhibition and fear aside and dive right in, God will take over and use us in ways we never dreamed possible. That idea that is burning a hole in your heart—it's time to stop dreaming about it, thinking about it, and talking about it. It's time to just do it!

What is holding you back from going after your dream?
Write out a prayer asking God to give you the courage
to overcome your fears.

_____

_____

_____

_____

_____

_____

_____

_____

_____

_____

_____

_____

_____

_____

_____

_____

What steps can you take this week to get started? It may mean clearing your schedule, stepping down from other responsibilities, and making yourself available and focused to pour into your dream.

_____

_____

_____

_____

_____

_____

_____

_____

_____

_____

_____

_____

_____

_____

_____

_____

Use this page and the next to write out your dream in its entirety. Commit it to the Lord and ask Him to write your story and use it for His glory.

_____

_____

_____

_____

_____

_____

_____

_____

_____

_____

_____

_____

_____

_____

_____

_____

_____

Acknowledgments

To my Savior, Jesus Christ, the author of my story: thank You for breathing life, hope, and dreams into my soul. My heart will always overflow with love and gratitude for ALL You have done for me!

Robb: thank you for being the best friend, supporter and husband I could ever have. I love our family and living out our dreams together! You have my heart forever!

Emma: it is such a privilege to be your mommy, and I am just smitten with you! I pray you always live for Jesus. God has big dreams for you sweet girl, and I can't wait to watch them unfold and to cheer you on! I love you forever!

Mom and Dad: there are not enough words to express my gratitude for all you have done for me! You took me in and loved me as your very own and literally changed the course of my life. God can't help but smile at your love and life of service to Him! I love you both with all my heart!

Ken and Peg, Steve and Michaelle: I am so blessed to have you in my life and to be in your amazing family! Thank you for loving me and supporting my dreams from the moment you met me! I know without a doubt that every life that is impacted from this book is a direct result of your prayers and support. I love you all dearly!

Bobby and Risa: you are not just part of my family and my story but a part of my heart forever. I love you both always and am proud to be your sister.

My dearest friends: you know who you are! Each of you have encouraged me, believed in me, laughed with me, cried with me, and cheered me on with this crazy dream of writing a book! I love doing life with each of you, and my life is richer because of it!

The pastors, women's ministry directors, and Amway leaders who have brought me in throughout the years to sing and speak: I thank you all from the bottom of my heart. You all believed in me and gave me the opportunity to live out my dreams! I am forever grateful to all of you.

Brooke Boling: thank you for packaging this book so beautifully. You are so gifted. As always, I love your work!

Esther Fedorkevich, Layce Smith, and the entire team at Fedd Books: thank you so much for ALL you have done to make this book a reality. I can't wait to see how God uses all of our efforts to impact lives. You all are awesome!

Notes

Chapter 4: Scaling the Mountains

1. Everest, directed by Greg MacGillivray, Stephen Judson, David Breashears, narrated by Liam Neeson. (1998; MacGillivray Freeman Films/Mirimax, 1999), DVD.

2. Wikipedia contributors, Everest (1998 film), Wikipedia, The Free Encyclopedia. 8 Aug. 2.

3. John Maxwell, Your Bridge to a Better Future (Nashville, Thomas Nelson, 1997), 142.

4. Colonel Harland Sanders, The Autobiography of the Original Celebrity Chef (Louisville, KFC Corporation, 2012), http://colonelsanders.com/images/pdf/COLONELS_JOURNEY_Full_Eng.pdf.

5. "Abraham Lincoln: Life Before the Presidency," The Miller Center, accessed December 19, 2014, http://millercenter.org/president/lincoln/essays/biography/2.

6. Nathan Furr, "How Failure Taught Edison to Repeatedly Innovate," Forbes. Last modified June 9, 2011, http://www.forbes.com/sites/nathanfurr/2011/06/09/how-failure-taught-edison-to-repeatedly-innovate/.

Chapter 5: This Will I Choose

7. Figure 1: Chart modified from [iBelieve.com, Inspirations, "You say, God says" chart] http://www.ibelieve.com/inspirations/you-say-god-says.html (accessed December 1, 2014). This chart was originally viewed by me on Ann Voskamp's website, Aholyexpereience.com, in a blog posted on January 23, 2014. A series of inquires led me to iBelieve.com as the potential original source. Therefore, iBelieve.com is the entity I have given credit to.

Chapter 7: Faith to Believe

8. *The Merriam-Webster Dictionary* (New York, Pocket

Books, 1974), 255.

9. Jud Wilhite, *Faith that Goes the Distance* (Grand Rapids, Baker Books, 2002), 26.

10. Lawrence Richards, The 365 Day Devotional Commentary (Wheaton, Victor Books, 1990), 336-337.

11. Lawrence Richards, The 365 Day Devotional Commentary (Wheaton, Victor Books, 1990), 337.

12. Jud Wilhite, Faith that Goes the Distance (Grand Rapids, Baker Books, 2002), 27.

13. Jud Wilhite, Faith that Goes the Distance (Grand Rapids, Baker Books, 2002), 103.

14. Every day when I wake up: Quote by Cheryl McGuiness.

Chapter 8: The Road Less Traveled

15. *The Merriam-Webster Dictionary* (New York, Pocket Books, 1974), 372.

16. Lysa Terkeurst, *The Best Yes* (Nashville, Thomas Nelson, 2014), 24.

Chapter 9: The Time is Now

17. John Maxwell, *The 21 Irrefutable Laws of Leadership* (Nashville, Thomas Nelson, 1998), 178.

18. Francis Chan, *Crazy Love* (Colorado Springs, David C. Cook, 2008), 93, quote by Tim Kizzair.

19. Mark Batterson, *All In* (Grand Rapids, Zondervan, 2013), 85-86.

Chapter 10: Just Do It

20. John Maxwell, *Your Bridge to a Better Future* (Nashville, Thomas Nelson, 1997), 12.

21. Paula Dunn, *Dare to Dream* (Paula Dunn Ministries, 2001).

About the Author
PAULA DUNN

For the past 28 years, Paula Dunn has been using her dynamic voice and her unique story to encourage, challenge, and inspire audiences of all ages. She began performing concerts at the age of 14 and has released 12 solo albums since then. Paula is a graduate of Liberty University where she received a BA in vocal performance and an MA in counseling.

Paula has been married to Robb for 18 years and has a beautiful 7-year-old daughter named Emma Grace. She makes Lynchburg, Virginia, her home. When not traveling with her ministry, Paula spends her days fixing meals, keeping up with housework and laundry, and spending time with those she loves. And if you really want to get personal, Paula loves sweet tea, dessert, and long walks to work it all off.

Paula's ministry was born out of a desire to help those who are hurting and to challenge people to rise above the obstacles in their lives. She often shares humorous, real life stories of being a wife and a mother and learning how to juggle the responsibilities of family, ministry, and living out God's dreams for our lives.

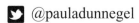